OAE

Mathematics (027)
Secrets Study Guide

Part 2 of 2

DEAR FUTURE EXAM SUCCESS STORY

First of all, **THANK YOU** for purchasing Mometrix study materials!

Second, congratulations! You are one of the few determined test-takers who are committed to doing whatever it takes to excel on your exam. **You have come to the right place.** We developed these study materials with one goal in mind: to deliver you the information you need in a format that's concise and easy to use.

In addition to optimizing your guide for the content of the test, we've outlined our recommended steps for breaking down the preparation process into small, attainable goals so you can make sure you stay on track.

We've also analyzed the entire test-taking process, identifying the most common pitfalls and showing how you can overcome them and be ready for any curveball the test throws you.

Standardized testing is one of the biggest obstacles on your road to success, which only increases the importance of doing well in the high-pressure, high-stakes environment of test day. Your results on this test could have a significant impact on your future, and this guide provides the information and practical advice to help you achieve your full potential on test day.

Your success is our success

We would love to hear from you! If you would like to share the story of your exam success or if you have any questions or comments in regard to our products, please contact us at **800-673-8175** or **support@mometrix.com**.

Thanks again for your business and we wish you continued success!

Sincerely,
The Mometrix Test Preparation Team

Need more help? Check out our flashcards at:
http://MometrixFlashcards.com/OAE

TABLE OF CONTENTS

Statistics, Probability, and Discrete Mathematics

Probability

PROBABILITY

Probability is the likelihood of a certain outcome occurring for a given event. An **event** is any situation that produces a result. It could be something as simple as flipping a coin or as complex as launching a rocket. Determining the probability of an outcome for an event can be equally simple or complex. As such, there are specific terms used in the study of probability that need to be understood:

- **Compound event**—an event that involves two or more independent events (rolling a pair of dice and taking the sum)
- **Desired outcome** (or success)—an outcome that meets a particular set of criteria (a roll of 1 or 2 if we are looking for numbers less than 3)
- **Independent events**—two or more events whose outcomes do not affect one another (two coins tossed at the same time)
- **Dependent events**—two or more events whose outcomes affect one another (two cards drawn consecutively from the same deck)
- **Certain outcome**—probability of outcome is 100% or 1
- **Impossible outcome**—probability of outcome is 0% or 0
- **Mutually exclusive outcomes**—two or more outcomes whose criteria cannot all be satisfied in a single event (a coin coming up heads and tails on the same toss)
- **Random variable**—refers to all possible outcomes of a single event which may be discrete or continuous.

> **Review Video: Intro to Probability**
> Visit mometrix.com/academy and enter code: 212374

THEORETICAL AND EXPERIMENTAL PROBABILITY

Theoretical probability can usually be determined without actually performing the event. The likelihood of an outcome occurring, or the probability of an outcome occurring, is given by the formula:

$$P(A) = \frac{\text{Number of acceptable outcomes}}{\text{Number of possible outcomes}}$$

Note that $P(A)$ is the probability of an outcome A occurring, and each outcome is just as likely to occur as any other outcome. If each outcome has the same probability of occurring as every other possible outcome, the outcomes are said to be equally likely to occur. The total number of acceptable outcomes must be less than or equal to the total number of possible outcomes. If the two are equal, then the outcome is certain to occur and the probability is 1. If the number of acceptable outcomes is zero, then the outcome is impossible and the probability is 0. For example, if there are 20 marbles in a bag and 5 are red, then the theoretical probability of randomly selecting a red marble is 5 out of 20, $\left(\frac{5}{20} = \frac{1}{4}, 0.25, \text{or } 25\%\right)$.

1

If the theoretical probability is unknown or too complicated to calculate, it can be estimated by an experimental probability. **Experimental probability**, also called empirical probability, is an estimate of the likelihood of a certain outcome based on repeated experiments or collected data. In other words, while theoretical probability is based on what *should* happen, experimental probability is based on what *has* happened. Experimental probability is calculated in the same way as theoretical probability, except that actual outcomes are used instead of possible outcomes. The more experiments performed or datapoints gathered, the better the estimate should be.

Theoretical and experimental probability do not always line up with one another. Theoretical probability says that out of 20 coin-tosses, 10 should be heads. However, if we were actually to toss 20 coins, we might record just 5 heads. This doesn't mean that our theoretical probability is incorrect; it just means that this particular experiment had results that were different from what was predicted. A practical application of empirical probability is the insurance industry. There are no set functions that define lifespan, health, or safety. Insurance companies look at factors from hundreds of thousands of individuals to find patterns that they then use to set the formulas for insurance premiums.

> **Review Video: Empirical Probability**
> Visit mometrix.com/academy and enter code: 513468

OBJECTIVE AND SUBJECTIVE PROBABILITY

Objective probability is based on mathematical formulas and documented evidence. Examples of objective probability include raffles or lottery drawings where there is a pre-determined number of possible outcomes and a predetermined number of outcomes that correspond to an event. Other cases of objective probability include probabilities of rolling dice, flipping coins, or drawing cards. Most gambling games are based on objective probability.

In contrast, **subjective probability** is based on personal or professional feelings and judgments. Often, there is a lot of guesswork following extensive research. Areas where subjective probability is applicable include sales trends and business expenses. Attractions set admission prices based on subjective probabilities of attendance based on varying admission rates in an effort to maximize their profit.

SAMPLE SPACE

The total set of all possible results of a test or experiment is called a **sample space**, or sometimes a universal sample space. The sample space, represented by one of the variables S, Ω, or U (for universal sample space) has individual elements called outcomes. Other terms for outcome that may be used interchangeably include elementary outcome, simple event, or sample point. The number of outcomes in a given sample space could be infinite or finite, and some tests may yield multiple unique sample sets. For example, tests conducted by drawing playing cards from a standard deck would have one sample space of the card values, another sample space of the card suits, and a third sample space of suit-denomination combinations. For most tests, the sample spaces considered will be finite.

An **event**, represented by the variable E, is a portion of a sample space. It may be one outcome or a group of outcomes from the same sample space. If an event occurs, then the test or experiment will generate an outcome that satisfies the requirement of that event. For example, given a standard deck of 52 playing cards as the sample space, and defining the event as the collection of face cards, then the event will occur if the card drawn is a J, Q, or K. If any other card is drawn, the event is said to have not occurred.

For every sample space, each possible outcome has a specific likelihood, or probability, that it will occur. The probability measure, also called the **distribution**, is a function that assigns a real number probability, from zero to one, to each outcome. For a probability measure to be accurate, every outcome must have a real number probability measure that is greater than or equal to zero and less than or equal to one. Also, the probability measure of the sample space must equal one, and the probability measure of the union of multiple outcomes must equal the sum of the individual probability measures.

Probabilities of events are expressed as real numbers from zero to one. They give a numerical value to the chance that a particular event will occur. The probability of an event occurring is the sum of the probabilities of the individual elements of that event. For example, in a standard deck of 52 playing cards as the sample space and the collection of face cards as the event, the probability of drawing a specific face card is $\frac{1}{52} = 0.019$, but the probability of drawing any one of the twelve face cards is $12(0.019) = 0.228$. Note that rounding of numbers can generate different results. If you multiplied 12 by the fraction $\frac{1}{52}$ before converting to a decimal, you would get the answer $\frac{12}{52} = 0.231$.

TREE DIAGRAM

For a simple sample space, possible outcomes may be determined by using a **tree diagram** or an organized chart. In either case, you can easily draw or list out the possible outcomes. For example, to determine all the possible ways three objects can be ordered, you can draw a tree diagram:

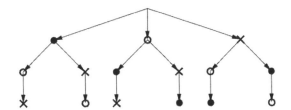

You can also make a chart to list all the possibilities:

First object	Second object	Third object
●	X	O
●	O	X
O	●	X
O	X	●
X	●	O
X	O	●

Either way, you can easily see there are six possible ways the three objects can be ordered.

If two events have no outcomes in common, they are said to be **mutually exclusive**. For example, in a standard deck of 52 playing cards, the event of all card suits is mutually exclusive to the event of all card values. If two events have no bearing on each other so that one event occurring has no influence on the probability of another event occurring, the two events are said to be independent. For example, rolling a standard six-sided die multiple times does not change that probability that a particular number will be rolled from one roll to the next. If the outcome of one event does affect

3

the probability of the second event, the two events are said to be dependent. For example, if cards are drawn from a deck, the probability of drawing an ace after an ace has been drawn is different than the probability of drawing an ace if no ace (or no other card, for that matter) has been drawn.

In probability, the **odds in favor of an event** are the number of times the event will occur compared to the number of times the event will not occur. To calculate the odds in favor of an event, use the formula $\frac{P(A)}{1-P(A)}$, where $P(A)$ is the probability that the event will occur. Many times, odds in favor is given as a ratio in the form $\frac{a}{b}$ or $a:b$, where a is the probability of the event occurring and b is the complement of the event, the probability of the event not occurring. If the odds in favor are given as 2:5, that means that you can expect the event to occur two times for every 5 times that it does not occur. In other words, the probability that the event will occur is $\frac{2}{2+5} = \frac{2}{7}$.

In probability, the **odds against an event** are the number of times the event will not occur compared to the number of times the event will occur. To calculate the odds against an event, use the formula $\frac{1-P(A)}{P(A)}$, where $P(A)$ is the probability that the event will occur. Many times, odds against is given as a ratio in the form $\frac{b}{a}$ or $b:a$, where b is the probability the event will not occur (the complement of the event) and a is the probability the event will occur. If the odds against an event are given as 3:1, that means that you can expect the event to not occur 3 times for every one time it does occur. In other words, 3 out of every 4 trials will fail.

PERMUTATIONS AND COMBINATIONS

When trying to calculate the probability of an event using the $\frac{\text{desired outcomes}}{\text{total outcomes}}$ formula, you may frequently find that there are too many outcomes to individually count them. **Permutation** and **combination formulas** offer a shortcut to counting outcomes. A permutation is an arrangement of a specific number of a set of objects in a specific order. The number of **permutations** of r items given a set of n items can be calculated as $_nP_r = \frac{n!}{(n-r)!}$. Combinations are similar to permutations, except there are no restrictions regarding the order of the elements. While ABC is considered a different permutation than BCA, ABC and BCA are considered the same combination. The number of **combinations** of r items given a set of n items can be calculated as $_nC_r = \frac{n!}{r!(n-r)!}$ or $_nC_r = \frac{_nP_r}{r!}$.

Suppose you want to calculate how many different 5-card hands can be drawn from a deck of 52 cards. This is a combination since the order of the cards in a hand does not matter. There are 52 cards available, and 5 to be selected. Thus, the number of different hands is $_{52}C_5 = \frac{52!}{5! \times 47!} = 2{,}598{,}960$.

Review Video: Probability - Permutation and Combination
Visit mometrix.com/academy and enter code: 907664

UNION AND INTERSECTION OF TWO SETS OF OUTCOMES

If A and B are each a set of elements or outcomes from an experiment, then the **union** (symbol $\cup$) of the two sets is the set of elements found in set A or set B. For example, if $A = \{2, 3, 4\}$ and $B = \{3, 4, 5\}$, $A \cup B = \{2, 3, 4, 5\}$. Note that the outcomes 3 and 4 appear only once in the union. For statistical events, the union is equivalent to "or"; $P(A \cup B)$ is the same thing as $P(A$ or $B)$. The **intersection** (symbol $\cap$) of two sets is the set of outcomes common to both sets. For the above sets A and B, $A \cap B = \{3, 4\}$. For statistical events, the intersection is equivalent to "and"; $P(A \cap B)$ is the same thing as $P(A$ and $B)$. It is important to note that union and intersection operations commute. That is:

$$A \cup B = B \cup A \text{ and } A \cap B = B \cap A$$

COMPLEMENT OF AN EVENT

Sometimes it may be easier to calculate the possibility of something not happening, or the **complement of an event**. Represented by the symbol $\bar{A}$, the complement of A is the probability that event A does not happen. When you know the probability of event A occurring, you can use the formula $P(\bar{A}) = 1 - P(A)$, where $P(\bar{A})$ is the probability of event A not occurring, and $P(A)$ is the probability of event A occurring.

ADDITION RULE

The **addition rule** for probability is used for finding the probability of a compound event. Use the formula $P(A$ or $B) = P(A) + P(B) - P(A$ and $B)$, where $P(A$ and $B)$ is the probability of both events occurring to find the probability of a compound event. The probability of both events occurring at the same time must be subtracted to eliminate any overlap in the first two probabilities.

CONDITIONAL PROBABILITY

Given two events A and B, the **conditional probability** $P(A|B)$ is the probability that event A will occur, given that event B has occurred. The conditional probability cannot be calculated simply from $P(A)$ and $P(B)$; these probabilities alone do not give sufficient information to determine the conditional probability. It can, however, be determined if you are also given the probability of the intersection of events A and B, $P(A \cap B)$, the probability that events A and B both occur.

Specifically, $P(A|B) = \frac{P(A \cap B)}{P(B)}$. For instance, suppose you have a jar containing two red marbles and two blue marbles, and you draw two marbles at random. Consider event A being the event that the first marble drawn is red, and event B being the event that the second marble drawn is blue. $P(A)$ is $\frac{1}{2}$, and $P(A \cap B)$ is $\frac{1}{3}$. (The latter may not be obvious, but may be determined by finding the product of $\frac{1}{2}$ and $\frac{2}{3}$). Therefore $P(A|B) = \frac{1/3}{1/2} = \frac{2}{3}$.

CONDITIONAL PROBABILITY IN EVERYDAY SITUATIONS

Conditional probability often arises in everyday situations in, for example, estimating the risk or benefit of certain activities. The conditional probability of having a heart attack given that you exercise daily may be smaller than the overall probability of having a heart attack. The conditional probability of having lung cancer given that you are a smoker is larger than the overall probability of having lung cancer. Note that changing the order of the conditional probability changes the meaning: the conditional probability of having lung cancer given that you are a smoker is a very different thing from the probability of being a smoker given that you have lung cancer. In an

5

extreme case, suppose that a certain rare disease is caused only by eating a certain food, but even then, it is unlikely. Then the conditional probability of having that disease given that you eat the dangerous food is nonzero but low, but the conditional probability of having eaten that food given that you have the disease is 100%!

Review Video: Conditional Probability
Visit mometrix.com/academy and enter code: 397924

INDEPENDENCE

The conditional probability $P(A|B)$ is the probability that event A will occur given that event B occurs. If the two events are independent, we do not expect that whether or not event B occurs should have any effect on whether or not event A occurs. In other words, we expect $P(A|B) = P(A)$.

This can be proven using the usual equations for conditional probability and the joint probability of independent events. The conditional probability $P(A|B) = \frac{P(A \cap B)}{P(B)}$. If A and B are independent, then $P(A \cap B) = P(A)P(B)$. So $P(A|B) = \frac{P(A)P(B)}{P(B)} = P(A)$. By similar reasoning, if A and B are independent then $P(B|A) = P(B)$.

TWO-WAY FREQUENCY TABLES

If we have a two-way frequency table, it is generally a straightforward matter to read off the probabilities of any two events A and B, as well as the joint probability of both events occurring, $P(A \cap B)$. We can then find the conditional probability $P(A|B)$ by calculating $P(A|B) = \frac{P(A \cap B)}{P(B)}$. We could also check whether or not events are independent by verifying whether $P(A)P(B) = P(A \cap B)$.

For example, a certain store's recent T-shirt sales:

Color \ Size	Small	Medium	Large	Total
Blue	25	40	35	100
White	27	25	22	74
Black	8	23	15	46
Total	60	88	72	220

Suppose we want to find the conditional probability that a customer buys a black shirt (event A), given that the shirt he buys is size small (event B). From the table, the probability $P(B)$ that a customer buys a small shirt is $\frac{60}{220} = \frac{3}{11}$. The probability $P(A \cap B)$ that he buys a small, black shirt is $\frac{8}{220} = \frac{2}{55}$. The conditional probability $P(A|B)$ that he buys a black shirt, given that he buys a small shirt, is therefore $P(A|B) = \frac{2/55}{3/11} = \frac{2}{15}$.

Similarly, if we want to check whether the event a customer buys a blue shirt, A, is independent of the event that a customer buys a medium shirt, B. From the table, $P(A) = \frac{100}{220} = \frac{5}{11}$ and $P(B) = \frac{88}{220} = \frac{4}{10}$. Also, $P(A \cap B) = \frac{40}{220} = \frac{2}{11}$. Since $\left(\frac{5}{11}\right)\left(\frac{4}{10}\right) = \frac{20}{220} = \frac{1}{11}$, $P(A)P(B) = P(A \cap B)$ and these two events are indeed independent.

MULTIPLICATION RULE

The **multiplication rule** can be used to find the probability of two independent events occurring using the formula $P(A \text{ and } B) = P(A) \times P(B)$, where $P(A \text{ and } B)$ is the probability of two independent events occurring, $P(A)$ is the probability of the first event occurring, and $P(B)$ is the probability of the second event occurring.

The multiplication rule can also be used to find the probability of two dependent events occurring using the formula $P(A \text{ and } B) = P(A) \times P(B|A)$, where $P(A \text{ and } B)$ is the probability of two dependent events occurring and $P(B|A)$ is the probability of the second event occurring after the first event has already occurred. Before using the multiplication rule, you MUST first determine whether the two events are *dependent* or *independent*.

Use a **combination of the multiplication** rule and the rule of complements to find the probability that at least one outcome of the element will occur. This is given by the general formula $P(\text{at least one event occurring}) = 1 - P(\text{no outcomes occurring})$. For example, to find the probability that at least one even number will show when a pair of dice is rolled, find the probability that two odd numbers will be rolled (no even numbers) and subtract from one. You can always use a tree diagram or make a chart to list the possible outcomes when the sample space is small, such as in the dice-rolling example, but in most cases it will be much faster to use the multiplication and complement formulas.

> **Review Video: Multiplication Rule**
> Visit mometrix.com/academy and enter code: 782598

EXPECTED VALUE

Expected value is a method of determining the expected outcome in a random situation. It is a sum of the weighted probabilities of the possible outcomes. Multiply the probability of an event occurring by the weight assigned to that probability (such as the amount of money won or lost). A practical application of the expected value is to determine whether a game of chance is really fair. If the sum of the weighted probabilities is equal to zero, the game is generally considered fair because the player has a fair chance to at least break even. If the expected value is less than zero, then players lose more than they win. For example, a lottery drawing might allow the player to choose any three-digit number, 000–999. The probability of choosing the winning number is 1:1000. If it costs \$1 to play, and a winning number receives \$500, the expected value is $\left(-\$1 \times \frac{999}{1,000}\right) + \left(\$499 \times \frac{1}{1,000}\right) = -\$0.50$. You can expect to lose on average 50 cents for every dollar you spend.

> **Review Video: Expected Value**
> Visit mometrix.com/academy and enter code: 643554

EXPECTED VALUE AND SIMULATORS

A die roll simulator will show the results of n rolls of a die. The result of each die roll may be recorded. For example, suppose a die is rolled 100 times. All results may be recorded. The numbers of 1s, 2s, 3s, 4s, 5s, and 6s, may be counted. The experimental probability of rolling each number will equal the ratio of the frequency of the rolled number to the total number of rolls. As the number of rolls increases, or approaches infinity, the experimental probability will approach the theoretical probability of $\frac{1}{6}$. Thus, the expected value for the roll of a die is shown to be $\left(1 \times \frac{1}{6}\right) + \left(2 \times \frac{1}{6}\right) + \left(3 \times \frac{1}{6}\right) + \left(4 \times \frac{1}{6}\right) + \left(5 \times \frac{1}{6}\right) + \left(6 \times \frac{1}{6}\right)$, or 3.5.

PRACTICE

P1. Determine the theoretical probability of the following events:

(a) Rolling an even number on a regular 6-sided die.

(b) Not getting a red ball when selecting one from a bag of 3 red balls, 4 black balls, and 2 green balls.

(c) Rolling a standard die and then selecting a card from a standard deck that is less than the value rolled.

P2. There is a game of chance involving a standard deck of cards that has been shuffled and then laid on a table. The player wins $10 if they can turn over 2 cards of matching color (black or red), $50 for 2 cards with matching value (A-K), and $100 for 2 cards with both matching color and value. What is the expected value of playing this game?

P3. Today, there were two food options for lunch at a local college cafeteria. Given the following survey data, what is the probability that a junior selected at random from the sample had a sandwich?

	Freshman	Sophomore	Junior	Senior
Salad	15	12	27	36
Sandwich	24	40	43	35
Nothing	42	23	23	30

PRACTICE SOLUTIONS

P1. (a). The values on the faces of a regular die are 1, 2, 3, 4, 5, and 6. Since three of these are even numbers (2, 4, 6), The probability of rolling an even number is $\frac{3}{6} = \frac{1}{2} = 0.5 = 50\%$.

(b) The bag contains a total of 9 balls, 6 of which are not red, so the probability of selecting one non-red ball would be $\frac{6}{9} = \frac{2}{3} \cong 0.667 \cong 66.7\%$.

(c) In this scenario, we need to determine how many cards could satisfy the condition for each possible value of the die roll. If a one is rolled, there is no way to achieve the desired outcome, since no cards in a standard deck are less than 1. If a two is rolled, then any of the four aces would achieve the desired result. If a three is rolled, then either an ace or a two would satisfy

8

the condition, and so on. Note that any value on the die is equally likely to occur, meaning that the probability of each roll is $\frac{1}{6}$. Putting all this in a table can help:

Roll	Cards < Roll	Probability of Card	Probability of Event
1	-	$\frac{0}{52} = 0$	$\frac{1}{6} \times 0 = 0$
2	1	$\frac{4}{52} = \frac{1}{13}$	$\frac{1}{6} \times \frac{1}{13} = \frac{1}{78}$
3	1,2	$\frac{8}{52} = \frac{2}{13}$	$\frac{1}{6} \times \frac{2}{13} = \frac{2}{78}$
4	1,2,3	$\frac{12}{52} = \frac{3}{13}$	$\frac{1}{6} \times \frac{3}{13} = \frac{3}{78}$
5	1,2,3,4	$\frac{16}{52} = \frac{4}{13}$	$\frac{1}{6} \times \frac{4}{13} = \frac{4}{78}$
6	1,2,3,4,5	$\frac{20}{52} = \frac{5}{13}$	$\frac{1}{6} \times \frac{5}{13} = \frac{5}{78}$

Assuming that each value of the die is equally likely, then the probability of selecting a card less than the value of the die is the sum of the probabilities of each way to achieve the desired outcome: $\frac{0+1+2+3+4+5}{78} = \frac{15}{78} = \frac{5}{26} \cong 0.192 \cong 19.2\%$.

P2. First, determine the probability of each way of winning. In each case, the first card simply determines which of the remaining 51 cards in the deck correspond to a win. For the color of the cards to match, there are 25 cards remaining in the deck that match the color of the first, but one of the 25 also matches the value, so only 24 are left in this category. For the value of the cards to match, there are 3 cards remaining in the deck that match the value of the first, but one of the three also matches the color, so only 2 are left in this category. There is only one card in the deck that will match both the color and value. Finally, there are 24 cards left that don't match at all.

Now we can find the expected value of playing the game, where we multiply the value of each event by the probability it will occur and sum over all of them:

$$\$10 \times \frac{24}{51} = \$4.71$$

$$\$50 \times \frac{2}{51} = \$1.96$$

$$\$100 \times \frac{1}{51} = \$1.96$$

$$\$0 \times \frac{24}{51} = \$0$$

$$\$4.71 + \$1.96 + \$1.96 = \$8.63$$

This game therefore has an expected value of $8.63 each time you play, which means if the cost to play is less than $8.63 then you would, on average, *gain* money. However, if the cost to play is more than $8.63, then you would, on average, *lose* money.

P3. With two-way tables it is often most helpful to start by totaling the rows and columns:

	Freshman	Sophomore	Junior	Senior	Total
Salad	15	12	27	36	90
Sandwich	24	40	43	35	142
Nothing	42	23	23	30	118
Total	81	75	93	101	350

Since the question is focused on juniors, we can focus on that column. There was a total of 93 juniors surveyed and 43 of them had a sandwich for lunch. Thus, the probability that a junior selected at random had a sandwich would be $\frac{43}{93} \cong 0.462 \cong 46.2\%$.

Statistics

STATISTICS

Statistics is the branch of mathematics that deals with collecting, recording, interpreting, illustrating, and analyzing large amounts of **data**. The following terms are often used in the discussion of data and **statistics**:

- **Data** – the collective name for pieces of information (singular is datum)
- **Quantitative data** – measurements (such as length, mass, and speed) that provide information about quantities in numbers
- **Qualitative data** – information (such as colors, scents, tastes, and shapes) that cannot be measured using numbers
- **Discrete data** – information that can be expressed only by a specific value, such as whole or half numbers. (e.g., since people can be counted only in whole numbers, a population count would be discrete data.)
- **Continuous data** – information (such as time and temperature) that can be expressed by any value within a given range
- **Primary data** – information that has been collected directly from a survey, investigation, or experiment, such as a questionnaire or the recording of daily temperatures. (Primary data that has not yet been organized or analyzed is called **raw data**.)
- **Secondary data** – information that has been collected, sorted, and processed by the researcher
- **Ordinal data** – information that can be placed in numerical order, such as age or weight
- **Nominal data** – information that *cannot* be placed in numerical order, such as names or places

DATA COLLECTION

POPULATION

In statistics, the **population** is the entire collection of people, plants, etc., that data can be collected from. For example, a study to determine how well students in local schools perform on a standardized test would have a population of all the students enrolled in those schools, although a study may include just a small sample of students from each school. A **parameter** is a numerical value that gives information about the population, such as the mean, median, mode, or standard deviation. Remember that the symbol for the mean of a population is μ and the symbol for the standard deviation of a population is σ.

SAMPLE

A **sample** is a portion of the entire population. Whereas a parameter helped describe the population, a **statistic** is a numerical value that gives information about the sample, such as mean, median, mode, or standard deviation. Keep in mind that the symbols for mean and standard deviation are different when they are referring to a sample rather than the entire population. For a sample, the symbol for mean is $\bar{x}$ and the symbol for standard deviation is s. The mean and standard deviation of a sample may or may not be identical to that of the entire population due to a sample only being a subset of the population. However, if the sample is random and large enough, statistically significant values can be attained. Samples are generally used when the population is too large to justify including every element or when acquiring data for the entire population is impossible.

INFERENTIAL STATISTICS

Inferential statistics is the branch of statistics that uses samples to make predictions about an entire population. This type of statistic is often seen in political polls, where a sample of the population is questioned about a particular topic or politician to gain an understanding of the attitudes of the entire population of the country. Often, exit polls are conducted on election days using this method. Inferential statistics can have a large margin of error if you do not have a valid sample.

SAMPLING DISTRIBUTION

Statistical values calculated from various samples of the same size make up the **sampling distribution**. For example, if several samples of identical size are randomly selected from a large population and then the mean of each sample is calculated, the distribution of values of the means would be a sampling distribution.

The **sampling distribution of the mean** is the distribution of the sample mean, $\bar{x}$, derived from random samples of a given size. It has three important characteristics. First, the mean of the sampling distribution of the mean is equal to the mean of the population that was sampled. Second, assuming the standard deviation is non-zero, the standard deviation of the sampling distribution of the mean equals the standard deviation of the sampled population divided by the square root of the sample size. This is sometimes called the standard error. Finally, as the sample size gets larger, the sampling distribution of the mean gets closer to a normal distribution via the central limit theorem.

SURVEY STUDY

A **survey study** is a method of gathering information from a small group in an attempt to gain enough information to make accurate general assumptions about the population. Once a survey study is completed, the results are then put into a summary report.

Survey studies are generally in the format of surveys, interviews, or questionnaires as part of an effort to find opinions of a particular group or to find facts about a group.

It is important to note that the findings from a survey study are only as accurate as the sample chosen from the population.

CORRELATIONAL STUDIES

Correlational studies seek to determine how much one variable is affected by changes in a second variable. For example, correlational studies may look for a relationship between the amount of time a student spends studying for a test and the grade that student earned on the test or between student scores on college admissions tests and student grades in college.

It is important to note that correlational studies cannot show a cause and effect, but rather can show only that two variables are or are not potentially correlated.

EXPERIMENTAL STUDIES

Experimental studies take correlational studies one step farther, in that they attempt to prove or disprove a cause-and-effect relationship. These studies are performed by conducting a series of experiments to test the hypothesis. For a study to be scientifically accurate, it must have both an experimental group that receives the specified treatment and a control group that does not get the treatment. This is the type of study pharmaceutical companies do as part of drug trials for new medications. Experimental studies are only valid when the proper scientific method has been followed. In other words, the experiment must be well-planned and executed without bias in the

testing process, all subjects must be selected at random, and the process of determining which subject is in which of the two groups must also be completely random.

OBSERVATIONAL STUDIES

Observational studies are the opposite of experimental studies. In observational studies, the tester cannot change or in any way control all of the variables in the test. For example, a study to determine which gender does better in math classes in school is strictly observational. You cannot change a person's gender, and you cannot change the subject being studied. The big downfall of observational studies is that you have no way of proving a cause-and-effect relationship because you cannot control outside influences. Events outside of school can influence a student's performance in school, and observational studies cannot take that into consideration.

RANDOM SAMPLES

For most studies, a **random sample** is necessary to produce valid results. Random samples should not have any particular influence to cause sampled subjects to behave one way or another. The goal is for the random sample to be a **representative sample**, or a sample whose characteristics give an accurate picture of the characteristics of the entire population. To accomplish this, you must make sure you have a proper **sample size**, or an appropriate number of elements in the sample.

BIASES

In statistical studies, biases must be avoided. **Bias** is an error that causes the study to favor one set of results over another. For example, if a survey to determine how the country views the president's job performance only speaks to registered voters in the president's party, the results will be skewed because a disproportionately large number of responders would tend to show approval, while a disproportionately large number of people in the opposite party would tend to express disapproval. **Extraneous variables** are, as the name implies, outside influences that can affect the outcome of a study. They are not always avoidable but could trigger bias in the result.

Statistical Analysis

MEASURES OF CENTRAL TENDENCY

A **measure of central tendency** is a statistical value that gives a reasonable estimate for the center of a group of data. There are several different ways of describing the measure of central tendency. Each one has a unique way it is calculated, and each one gives a slightly different perspective on the data set. Whenever you give a measure of central tendency, always make sure the units are the same. If the data has different units, such as hours, minutes, and seconds, convert all the data to the same unit, and use the same unit in the measure of central tendency. If no units are given in the data, do not give units for the measure of central tendency.

MEAN

The **statistical mean** of a group of data is the same as the arithmetic average of that group. To find the mean of a set of data, first convert each value to the same units, if necessary. Then find the sum of all the values, and count the total number of data values, making sure you take into consideration each individual value. If a value appears more than once, count it more than once. Divide the sum of the values by the total number of values and apply the units, if any. Note that the mean does not have to be one of the data values in the set, and may not divide evenly.

$$\text{mean} = \frac{\text{sum of the data values}}{\text{quantity of data values}}$$

For instance, the mean of the data set {88, 72, 61, 90, 97, 68, 88, 79, 86, 93, 97, 71, 80, 84, 89} would be the sum of the fifteen numbers divided by 15:

$$\frac{88 + 72 + 61 + 90 + 97 + 68 + 88 + 79 + 86 + 93 + 97 + 71 + 80 + 84 + 88}{15} = \frac{1242}{15}$$
$$= 82.8$$

While the mean is relatively easy to calculate and averages are understood by most people, the mean can be very misleading if it is used as the sole measure of central tendency. If the data set has outliers (data values that are unusually high or unusually low compared to the rest of the data values), the mean can be very distorted, especially if the data set has a small number of values. If unusually high values are countered with unusually low values, the mean is not affected as much. For example, if five of twenty students in a class get a 100 on a test, but the other 15 students have an average of 60 on the same test, the class average would appear as 70. Whenever the mean is skewed by outliers, it is always a good idea to include the median as an alternate measure of central tendency.

A **weighted mean**, or weighted average, is a mean that uses "weighted" values. The formula is weighted mean $= \frac{w_1x_1+w_2x_2+w_3x_3...+w_nx_n}{w_1+w_2+w_3+\cdots+w_n}$. Weighted values, such as $w_1, w_2, w_3, ... w_n$ are assigned to each member of the set $x_1, x_2, x_3, ... x_n$. When calculating the weighted mean, make sure a weight value for each member of the set is used.

MEDIAN

The **statistical median** is the value in the middle of the set of data. To find the median, list all data values in order from smallest to largest or from largest to smallest. Any value that is repeated in the set must be listed the number of times it appears. If there are an odd number of data values, the median is the value in the middle of the list. If there is an even number of data values, the median is the arithmetic mean of the two middle values.

14

For example, the median of the data set {88, 72, 61, 90, 97, 68, 88, 79, 86, 93, 97, 71, 80, 84, 88} is 86 since the ordered set is {61, 68, 71, 72, 79, 80, 84, **86**, 88, 88, 88, 90, 93, 97, 97}.

The big disadvantage of using the median as a measure of central tendency is that is relies solely on a value's relative size as compared to the other values in the set. When the individual values in a set of data are evenly dispersed, the median can be an accurate tool. However, if there is a group of rather large values or a group of rather small values that are not offset by a different group of values, the information that can be inferred from the median may not be accurate because the distribution of values is skewed.

MODE

The **statistical mode** is the data value that occurs the greatest number of times in the data set. It is possible to have exactly one mode, more than one mode, or no mode. To find the mode of a set of data, arrange the data like you do to find the median (all values in order, listing all multiples of data values). Count the number of times each value appears in the data set. If all values appear an equal number of times, there is no mode. If one value appears more than any other value, that value is the mode. If two or more values appear the same number of times, but there are other values that appear fewer times and no values that appear more times, all of those values are the modes.

For example, the mode of the data set {**88**, 72, 61, 90, 97, 68, **88**, 79, 86, 93, 97, 71, 80, 84, **88**} is 88.

The main disadvantage of the mode is that the values of the other data in the set have no bearing on the mode. The mode may be the largest value, the smallest value, or a value anywhere in between in the set. The mode only tells which value or values, if any, occurred the greatest number of times. It does not give any suggestions about the remaining values in the set.

> **Review Video: All About Averages**
> Visit mometrix.com/academy and enter code: 176521
>
> **Review Video: Mean, Median, and Mode**
> Visit mometrix.com/academy and enter code: 286207

DISPERSION

A **measure of dispersion** is a single value that helps to "interpret" the measure of central tendency by providing more information about how the data values in the set are distributed about the measure of central tendency. The measure of dispersion helps to eliminate or reduce the disadvantages of using the mean, median, or mode as a single measure of central tendency, and give a more accurate picture of the dataset as a whole. To have a measure of dispersion, you must know or calculate the range, standard deviation, or variance of the data set.

RANGE

The **range** of a set of data is the difference between the greatest and lowest values of the data in the set. To calculate the range, you must first make sure the units for all data values are the same, and then identify the greatest and lowest values. If there are multiple data values that are equal for the highest or lowest, just use one of the values in the formula. Write the answer with the same units as the data values you used to do the calculations.

> **Review Video: Statistical Range**
> Visit mometrix.com/academy and enter code: 778541

STANDARD DEVIATION

Standard deviation is a measure of dispersion that compares all the data values in the set to the mean of the set to give a more accurate picture. To find the standard deviation of a sample, use the formula

$$s = \sqrt{\frac{\sum_{i=1}^{n}(x_i - \bar{x})^2}{n-1}}$$

Note that s is the standard deviation of a sample, x represents the individual values in the data set, $\bar{x}$ is the mean of the data values in the set, and n is the number of data values in the set. The higher the value of the standard deviation is, the greater the variance of the data values from the mean. The units associated with the standard deviation are the same as the units of the data values.

Review Video: Standard Deviation
Visit mometrix.com/academy and enter code: 419469

VARIANCE

The **variance** of a sample, or just variance, is the square of the standard deviation of that sample. While the mean of a set of data gives the average of the set and gives information about where a specific data value lies in relation to the average, the variance of the sample gives information about the degree to which the data values are spread out and tells you how close an individual value is to the average compared to the other values. The units associated with variance are the same as the units of the data values squared.

PERCENTILE

Percentiles and quartiles are other methods of describing data within a set. **Percentiles** tell what percentage of the data in the set fall below a specific point. For example, achievement test scores are often given in percentiles. A score at the 80th percentile is one which is equal to or higher than 80 percent of the scores in the set. In other words, 80 percent of the scores were lower than that score.

Quartiles are percentile groups that make up quarter sections of the data set. The first quartile is the 25th percentile. The second quartile is the 50th percentile; this is also the median of the dataset. The third quartile is the 75th percentile.

SKEWNESS

Skewness is a way to describe the symmetry or asymmetry of the distribution of values in a dataset. If the distribution of values is symmetrical, there is no skew. In general the closer the mean of a data set is to the median of the data set, the less skew there is. Generally, if the mean is to the right of the median, the data set is *positively skewed*, or right-skewed, and if the mean is to the left of the median, the data set is *negatively skewed*, or left-skewed. However, this rule of thumb is not infallible. When the data values are graphed on a curve, a set with no skew will be a perfect bell curve.

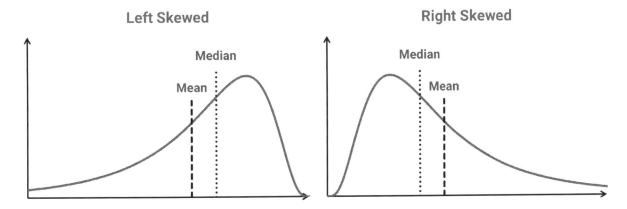

To estimate skew, use the formula:

$$\text{skew} = \frac{\sqrt{n(n-1)}}{n-2}\left(\frac{\frac{1}{n}\sum_{i-1}^{n}(x_i-\bar{x})^3}{\left(\frac{1}{n}\sum_{i=1}^{n}(x_i-\bar{x})^2\right)^{\frac{3}{2}}}\right)$$

Note that n is the datapoints in the set, x_i is the ith value in the set, and $\bar{x}$ is the mean of the set.

Review Video: Skew
Visit mometrix.com/academy and enter code: 661486

UNIMODAL VS. BIMODAL

If a distribution has a single peak, it would be considered **unimodal**. If it has two discernible peaks it would be considered **bimodal**. Bimodal distributions may be an indication that the set of data being considered is actually the combination of two sets of data with significant differences. A **uniform distribution** is a distribution in which there is *no distinct peak or variation* in the data. No values or ranges are particularly more common than any other values or ranges.

OUTLIER

An outlier is an extremely high or extremely low value in the data set. It may be the result of measurement error, in which case, the outlier is not a valid member of the data set. However, it may also be a valid member of the distribution. Unless a measurement error is identified, the experimenter cannot know for certain if an outlier is or is not a member of the distribution. There are arbitrary methods that can be employed to designate an extreme value as an outlier. One method designates an outlier (or possible outlier) to be any value less than $Q_1 - 1.5(IQR)$ or any value greater than $Q_3 + 1.5(IQR)$.

DATA ANALYSIS
SIMPLE REGRESSION

In statistics, **simple regression** is using an equation to represent a relation between independent and dependent variables. The independent variable is also referred to as the explanatory variable or the predictor and is generally represented by the variable x in the equation. The dependent variable, usually represented by the variable y, is also referred to as the response variable. The

17

equation may be any type of function – linear, quadratic, exponential, etc. The best way to handle this task is to use the regression feature of your graphing calculator. This will easily give you the curve of best fit and provide you with the coefficients and other information you need to derive an equation.

LINE OF BEST FIT

In a scatter plot, the **line of best fit** is the line that best shows the trends of the data. The line of best fit is given by the equation $\hat{y} = ax + b$, where a and b are the regression coefficients. The regression coefficient a is also the slope of the line of best fit, and b is also the y-coordinate of the point at which the line of best fit crosses the y-axis. Not every point on the scatter plot will be on the line of best fit. The differences between the y-values of the points in the scatter plot and the corresponding y-values according to the equation of the line of best fit are the residuals. The line of best fit is also called the least-squares regression line because it is also the line that has the lowest sum of the squares of the residuals.

CORRELATION COEFFICIENT

The **correlation coefficient** is the numerical value that indicates how strong the relationship is between the two variables of a linear regression equation. A correlation coefficient of –1 is a perfect negative correlation. A correlation coefficient of +1 is a perfect positive correlation. Correlation coefficients close to –1 or +1 are very strong correlations. A correlation coefficient equal to zero indicates there is no correlation between the two variables. This test is a good indicator of whether or not the equation for the line of best fit is accurate. The formula for the correlation coefficient is

$$r = \frac{\sum_{i=1}^{n}(x_i - \bar{x})(y_i - \bar{y})}{\sqrt{\sum_{i=1}^{n}(x_i - \bar{x})^2}\sqrt{\sum_{i=1}^{n}(y_i - \bar{y})^2}}$$

where r is the correlation coefficient, n is the number of data values in the set, (x_i, y_i) is a point in the set, and $\bar{x}$ and $\bar{y}$ are the means.

Z-SCORE

A **z-score** is an indication of how many standard deviations a given value falls from the mean. To calculate a z-score, use the formula:

$$\frac{x - \mu}{\sigma}$$

x is the data value, μ is the mean of the data set, and σ is the standard deviation of the population. If the z-score is positive, the data value lies above the mean. If the z-score is negative, the data value falls below the mean. These scores are useful in interpreting data such as standardized test scores, where every piece of data in the set has been counted, rather than just a small random sample. In cases where standard deviations are calculated from a random sample of the set, the z-scores will not be as accurate.

CENTRAL LIMIT THEOREM

According to the **central limit theorem**, regardless of what the original distribution of a sample is, the distribution of the means tends to get closer and closer to a normal distribution as the sample size gets larger and larger (this is necessary because the sample is becoming more all-encompassing of the elements of the population). As the sample size gets larger, the distribution of the sample mean will approach a normal distribution with a mean of the population mean and a variance of the population variance divided by the sample size.

PRACTICE

P1. Suppose the class average on a final exam is 87, with a standard deviation of 2 points. Find the z-score of a student that got an 82.

P2. Given the following graph, determine the range of patient ages:

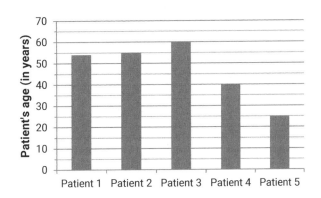

P3. Calculate the sample variance for the dataset $\{10, 13, 12, 5, 8, 18\}$

PRACTICE SOLUTIONS

P1. Using the formula for z-score: $z = \frac{82-87}{2} = -2.5$

P2. Patient 1 is 54 years old; Patient 2 is 55 years old; Patient 3 is 60 years old; Patient 4 is 40 years old; and Patient 5 is 25 years old. The range of patient ages is the age of the oldest patient minus the age of the youngest patient. In other words, $60 - 25 = 35$. The range of ages is 35 years.

P3. To find the variance, first find the mean:

$$\frac{10 + 13 + 12 + 5 + 8 + 18}{6} = \frac{66}{6} = 11$$

Now, apply the formula for sample variance:

$$
\begin{aligned}
s^2 &= \frac{\sum_{i=1}^{n}(x_i - \bar{x})^2}{n-1} = \frac{\sum_{i=1}^{6}(x_i - 11)^2}{6-1} \\
&= \frac{(10-11)^2 + (13-11)^2 + (12-11)^2 + (5-11)^2 + (8-11)^2 + (18-11)^2}{5} \\
&= \frac{(-1)^2 + 2^2 + 1^2 + (-6)^2 + (-3)^2 + 7^2}{5} \\
&= \frac{1 + 4 + 1 + 36 + 9 + 49}{5} \\
&= \frac{100}{5} = 20
\end{aligned}
$$

Displaying Information

FREQUENCY TABLES

Frequency tables show how frequently each unique value appears in a set. A **relative frequency table** is one that shows the proportions of each unique value compared to the entire set. Relative frequencies are given as percentages; however, the total percent for a relative frequency table will not necessarily equal 100 percent due to rounding. An example of a frequency table with relative frequencies is below.

Favorite Color	Frequency	Relative Frequency
Blue	4	13%
Red	7	22%
Green	3	9%
Purple	6	19%
Cyan	12	38%

> **Review Video: Data Interpretation of Graphs**
> Visit mometrix.com/academy and enter code: 200439

CIRCLE GRAPHS

Circle graphs, also known as *pie charts*, provide a visual depiction of the relationship of each type of data compared to the whole set of data. The circle graph is divided into sections by drawing radii to create central angles whose percentage of the circle is equal to the individual data's percentage of the whole set. Each 1% of data is equal to 3.6° in the circle graph. Therefore, data represented by a 90° section of the circle graph makes up 25% of the whole. When complete, a circle graph often looks like a pie cut into uneven wedges. The pie chart below shows the data from the frequency table referenced earlier where people were asked their favorite color.

Favorite Color

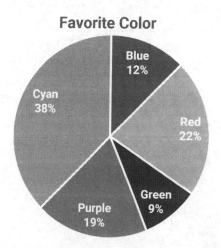

PICTOGRAPHS

A **pictograph** is a graph, generally in the horizontal orientation, that uses pictures or symbols to represent the data. Each pictograph must have a key that defines the picture or symbol and gives the quantity each picture or symbol represents. Pictures or symbols on a pictograph are not always shown as whole elements. In this case, the fraction of the picture or symbol shown represents the same fraction of the quantity a whole picture or symbol stands for. For example, a row with $3\frac{1}{2}$ ears

20

of corn, where each ear of corn represents 100 stalks of corn in a field, would equal $3\frac{1}{2} \times 100 = 350$ stalks of corn in the field.

> **Review Video: Pictographs**
> Visit mometrix.com/academy and enter code: 147860

LINE GRAPHS

Line graphs have one or more lines of varying styles (solid or broken) to show the different values for a set of data. The individual data are represented as ordered pairs, much like on a Cartesian plane. In this case, the x- and y-axes are defined in terms of their units, such as dollars or time. The individual plotted points are joined by line segments to show whether the value of the data is increasing (line sloping upward), decreasing (line sloping downward), or staying the same (horizontal line). Multiple sets of data can be graphed on the same line graph to give an easy visual comparison. An example of this would be graphing achievement test scores for different groups of students over the same time period to see which group had the greatest increase or decrease in performance from year to year (as shown below).

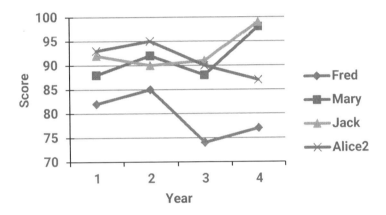

> **Review Video: How to Create a Line Graph**
> Visit mometrix.com/academy and enter code: 480147

LINE PLOTS

A **line plot**, also known as a *dot plot*, has plotted points that are not connected by line segments. In this graph, the horizontal axis lists the different possible values for the data, and the vertical axis lists the number of times the individual value occurs. A single dot is graphed for each value to show the number of times it occurs. This graph is more closely related to a bar graph than a line graph. Do not connect the dots in a line plot or it will misrepresent the data.

> **Review Video: Line Plot**
> Visit mometrix.com/academy and enter code: 754610

STEM AND LEAF PLOTS

A **stem and leaf plot** is useful for depicting groups of data that fall into a range of values. Each piece of data is separated into two parts: the first, or left, part is called the stem; the second, or right, part is called the leaf. Each stem is listed in a column from smallest to largest. Each leaf that has the common stem is listed in that stem's row from smallest to largest. For example, in a set of two-digit

21

numbers, the digit in the tens place is the stem, and the digit in the ones place is the leaf. With a stem and leaf plot, you can easily see which subset of numbers (10s, 20s, 30s, etc.) is the largest. This information is also readily available by looking at a histogram, but a stem and leaf plot also allows you to look closer and see exactly which values fall in that range. Using all of the test scores from above, we can assemble a stem and leaf plot like the one below.

Test Scores

7	4	8						
8	2	5	7	8	8			
9	0	0	1	2	2	3	5	8	9

> **Review Video: Stem and Leaf Plots**
> Visit mometrix.com/academy and enter code: 302339

BAR GRAPHS

A **bar graph** is one of the few graphs that can be drawn correctly in two different configurations – both horizontally and vertically. A bar graph is similar to a line plot in the way the data is organized on the graph. Both axes must have their categories defined for the graph to be useful. Rather than placing a single dot to mark the point of the data's value, a bar, or thick line, is drawn from zero to the exact value of the data, whether it is a number, percentage, or other numerical value. Longer bar lengths correspond to greater data values. To read a bar graph, read the labels for the axes to find the units being reported. Then, look where the bars end in relation to the scale given on the corresponding axis and determine the associated value.

The bar chart below represents the responses from our favorite-color survey.

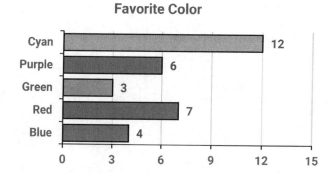

HISTOGRAMS

At first glance, a **histogram** looks like a vertical bar graph. The difference is that a bar graph has a separate bar for each piece of data and a histogram has one continuous bar for each *range* of data. For example, a histogram may have one bar for the range 0–9, one bar for 10–19, etc. While a bar graph has numerical values on one axis, a histogram has numerical values on both axes. Each range is of equal size, and they are ordered left to right from lowest to highest. The height of each column on a histogram represents the number of data values within that range. Like a stem and leaf plot, a histogram makes it easy to glance at the graph and quickly determine which range has the greatest quantity of values. A simple example of a histogram is below.

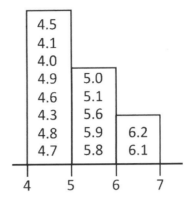

BIVARIATE DATA

Bivariate data is simply data from two different variables. (The prefix *bi-* means *two*.) In a *scatter plot*, each value in the set of data is plotted on a grid similar to a Cartesian plane, where each axis represents one of the two variables. By looking at the pattern formed by the points on the grid, you can often determine whether or not there is a relationship between the two variables, and what that relationship is, if it exists. The variables may be directly proportionate, inversely proportionate, or show no proportion at all. It may also be possible to determine if the data is linear, and if so, to find an equation to relate the two variables. The following scatter plot shows the relationship between preference for brand "A" and the age of the consumers surveyed.

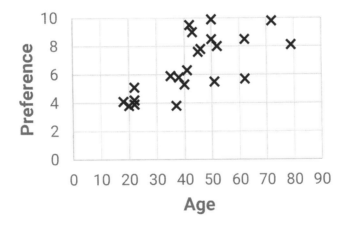

SCATTER PLOTS

Scatter plots are also useful in determining the type of function represented by the data and finding the simple regression. Linear scatter plots may be positive or negative. Nonlinear scatter plots are generally exponential or quadratic. Below are some common types of scatter plots:

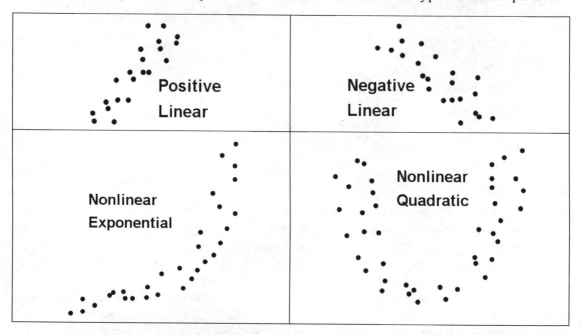

Positive Linear	Negative Linear
Nonlinear Exponential	Nonlinear Quadratic

Review Video: What is a Scatter Plot?
Visit mometrix.com/academy and enter code: 596526

5-NUMBER SUMMARY

The **5-number summary** of a set of data gives a very informative picture of the set. The five numbers in the summary include the minimum value, maximum value, and the three quartiles. This information gives the reader the range and median of the set, as well as an indication of how the data is spread about the median.

BOX AND WHISKER PLOTS

A **box-and-whiskers plot** is a graphical representation of the 5-number summary. To draw a box-and-whiskers plot, plot the points of the 5-number summary on a number line. Draw a box whose ends are through the points for the first and third quartiles. Draw a vertical line in the box through the median to divide the box in half. Draw a line segment from the first quartile point to the minimum value, and from the third quartile point to the maximum value.

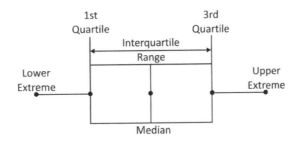

68-95-99.7 RULE

The **68–95–99.7 rule** describes how a normal distribution of data should appear when compared to the mean. This is also a description of a normal bell curve. According to this rule, 68 percent of the data values in a normally distributed set should fall within one standard deviation of the mean (34 percent above and 34 percent below the mean), 95 percent of the data values should fall within two standard deviations of the mean (47.5 percent above and 47.5 percent below the mean), and 99.7 percent of the data values should fall within three standard deviations of the mean, again, equally distributed on either side of the mean. This means that only 0.3 percent of all data values should fall more than three standard deviations from the mean. On the graph below, the normal curve is centered on the y-axis. The x-axis labels are how many standard deviations away from the center you are. Therefore, it is easy to see how the 68-95-99.7 rule can apply.

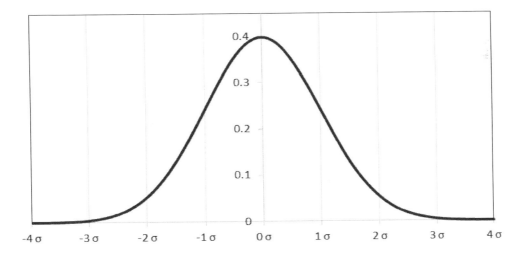

Discrete Mathematics

DISCRETE MATHEMATICS

Among mathematicians, there is not an agreed-upon definition of discrete math. What is agreed upon is the fact that discrete math deals with processes that use a finite, or countable, number of elements. In discrete math, the elements will be discontinuous, as this branch of mathematics does not involve the continuity that processes of calculus do. Generally, discrete math uses countable sets of rational numbers, although they do not use the set of all real numbers, as that would then make the math continuous and put it in the category of algebra or calculus. Discrete math has numerous applications in the fields of computer science and business.

ELEMENT OF A SET

A set is a mathematical collection of items, and an element is an item that is included in the set. These items are typically sets of numbers, or sets of geometrical points, or even sets of sets.

Whether an item is an **element of a set** is a binary property. In other words, a particular item either is or is not an element of a given set. There are not different degrees of belonging to a set, and one element of a set cannot be more an element than another. Additionally, the elements do not have any particular order, and there is no count of how many times an element appears in a set. For example, in the set $\{0, 2, 1, 2, 4\}$, the numbers 0, 1, 2, and 4 are elements of the set. Two is not more of an element than the others because it is listed twice. Any number other than these, such as 3, is not an element of the set.

The mathematical symbol $\in$ means "is an element of." for instance, "$1 \in A$" means that "the number 1 is an element of set A". The symbol can be negated with a diagonal slash, so "$1 \notin A$" means "the number 1 is *not* an element of set A."

EMPTY SET

The empty set contains no elements. The symbol for the **empty set** is a circle with a line through it, $\emptyset$, or the empty set can be written in roster form as $\{\ \}$. Although it may seem trivial, the empty set is important for the same reason that zero is an important number—without the empty set, many set operations and definitions would be incomplete. For instance, the intersection of two non-overlapping sets is the empty set. The set of all prime numbers that are perfect squares is the empty set, because there are no such numbers. Other sets can be constructed using the empty set. For instance, a set *containing* the empty set, $\{\{\ \}\}$ or $\{\emptyset\}$, is different from the empty set itself, since it's not actually empty—it contains one element, the empty set.

The empty set is, by definition, a subset of every set, including itself. This is because every element that is an element of the empty set is also an element of any other set, since the empty set contains no elements that could make this statement false.

SUBSET, PROPER SUBSET, AND SUPERSET

Set A is a **subset** of set B if set A is contained entirely within set B. More formally, set A is a subset of set B if every element of set A is also in set B. We can write this as $\forall x (x \in A \Rightarrow x \in B)$. The symbol for subset is $\subseteq$, so we can write "$A \subseteq B$" to mean "set A is a subset of set B," or "$A \nsubseteq B$" to mean "set A is NOT a subset of set B".

Any set is a subset of itself, since naturally any element in a set is in that set. A **proper subset** means a subset that is not equal to the other set. In other words, set A is a proper subset of set B if set A is a subset of set B but they are not the same, so $A \subseteq B$ but $B \nsubseteq A$. For example, $\{0, 1, 2\}$ is a proper subset of $\{0, 1, 2, 3\}$ because every element in the first set is included in the second set but the two sets are not identical. The symbol for a proper subset is $\subset$, so we write "$A \subset B$" to mean "set A is a proper subset of set B," and "$A \not\subset B$" to mean "set A is not a proper subset of set B."

The converse of a subset is a **superset**. If A is a subset of B, then B is a superset of A. In the example above, $\{0, 1, 2, 3\}$ is a superset of $\{0, 1, 2\}$ because the first set contains every element of the second plus more.

UNION OF TWO OR MORE SETS

The **union** of two or more sets includes all the elements that are included in all of the sets. An element is in the union of sets A and B if it is in set A or in set B, or in both. The union is written with the symbol $\cup$, so "$A \cup B$" (read "A union B") means the union of sets A and B.

For example, given the sets $A = \{1, 2, 3, 4\}$ and $B = \{2, 4, 6, 8\}$, then $A \cup B = \{1, 2, 3, 4, 6, 8\}$. 1 and 3 are in $A \cup B$ because they are in set A, and 6 and 8 are in $A \cup B$ because they are in set B. 2 and 4 appear in both A and B, so they are in $A \cup B$, but they only appear once.

The union operation on sets is both commutative and associative. That is, $A \cup B = B \cup A$, and $(A \cup B) \cup C = A \cup (B \cup C)$.

INTERSECTION OF TWO OR MORE SETS

The intersection of two or more sets is a set including every element that appears in *all* of the sets. An element is in the intersection of sets A and B if and only if, the element appears in both set A and set B. For instance, if set $A = \{0, 1, 2, 3\}$ and set $B = \{2, 3, 4, 5\}$, the intersection of sets A and B includes the elements 2 and 3, because these are the only elements that appear in both sets. The intersection is written with the symbol $\cap$, so "$A \cap B$" (read "A intersection B") means the intersection of sets A and B.

The intersection operation on sets is both commutative and associative. That is, $A \cap B = B \cap A$, and $(A \cap B) \cap C = A \cap (B \cap C)$. The union and intersection operations also jointly have distributive properties: $A \cap (B \cup C) = (A \cap B) \cup (A \cap C)$ and $A \cup (B \cap C) = (A \cup B) \cap (A \cup C)$.

COMPLEMENT OF A SET

The complement of a set is a set containing all the elements that are *not* in the original set. To determine this, we must also define the **universe of discourse**—the set of all possible elements we're considering, abbreviated U. For mathematical applications, the universe of discourse is commonly the set of all integers (abbreviated $\mathbb{Z}$), or the set of all real numbers (abbreviated $\mathbb{R}$). If U is the set of all integers, for example, then the complement of the set $A = \{1, 2, 3\}$ would include elements such as -3, 0, or 6, but it would not include elements such as $\sqrt{7}$ or $\frac{1}{4}$, because these are not in the universe of discourse.

The **complement of a set** is often written either by drawing a line over the name of the original set, or by adding an apostrophe or a superscripted C. The complement of set A, for instance, could be written as $\bar{A}$, as A', or as A^C.

For example, given set $A = \{2, 4, 6, 8\}$ with a universe of discourse of $U = \{1, 2, 3, 4, 5, 6, 7, 8, 9, 10\}$, the complement of set A would be $\{1, 3, 5, 7, 9, 10\}$—all the elements of U that are not in A.

DIFFERENCE OF TWO SETS

The difference of two sets is a set containing all the elements that are in the first set but not in the second. The difference of sets A and B is also referred to as the **relative complement** of set A with

27

respect to set B, and is written $A \setminus B$ or $A - B$. The difference is always a subset of the first set: $A \setminus B \subseteq A$. However, it is *not* necessarily the case that $A \setminus B \subseteq B$. In fact, because any element of $A \setminus B$ is by definition not an element of B, the only time that $A \setminus B$ can be a subset of B is if $A \setminus B$ has no elements, i.e., if $A \setminus B = \emptyset$, which is true if and only if, $A \subseteq B$.

Unlike the union and intersection, the operation of the difference between sets is neither commutative nor associative. In general, $A \setminus B \neq B \setminus A$, and $A \setminus (B \setminus C) \neq (A \setminus B) \setminus C$.

For example, consider the sets $A = \{1, 2, 3\}$, $B = \{2, 4\}$, and $C = \{1, 2\}$. Then $A \setminus B = \{1, 3\}$ since 1 and 3 are in set A but not in set B. Similarly, $B \setminus A = \{4\}$, $B \setminus C = \{4\}$, $C \setminus B = \{1\}$, and $A \setminus C = \{3\}$. However, $C \setminus A = \emptyset$, i.e., set C is a subset of set A, so there are no elements that appear in C but not in A, which means the difference between C and A is the empty set.

Symbols for Sets Commonly Used in Mathematics

Certain sets are used frequently enough in mathematics to have their own symbols. The standard symbols for these sets resemble upper-case letters of the Latin alphabet, but in a typeface with double lines. Among the most commonly used **sets** are:

- $\mathbb{R}$ – the set of all real numbers
- $\mathbb{Z}$ – the set of all integers
- $\mathbb{N}$ – the set of all natural numbers
- $\mathbb{Q}$ – the set of all rational numbers (numbers that can be written as the ratio of two integers, $\frac{p}{q}$, where $q \neq 0$)
- $\mathbb{C}$ – the set of all complex numbers (numbers of the form $a + bi$, where a and b are real numbers and $i = \sqrt{-1}$)

A superscripted plus or minus sign is used to restrict the set to positive or negative numbers. for instance, $\mathbb{R}^+$ would be the set of all positive real numbers, and $\mathbb{Z}^-$ would be the set of all negative integers.

Some of these sets are, of course, subsets of others. Specifically, $\mathbb{N} \subset \mathbb{Z} \subset \mathbb{Q} \subset \mathbb{R} \subset \mathbb{C}$.

Representing Sets with Recursive and Explicit Formulas

Sets of numbers can have a consistent relationship between the elements of the set. Some of these relationships can be represented with simple recursive or explicit formulas. For example, consider the set of all positive, even numbers (a) and the set of all positive, odd numbers (b):

Positive, even numbers:
Recursive: $a_n = a_{n-1} + 2, n \geq 2, a_1 = 0$
Explicit: $a_n = 2n, n \geq 0$

Positive, odd numbers:
Recursive: $b_n = b_{n-1} + 2, n \geq 2, b_1 = 1$
Explicit: $b_n = 2n + 1, n \geq 0$

Each set of numbers represents a linear function, with a constant rate of change of 2. The positive, even numbers represent a linear function that is proportional, whereas the positive, odd numbers represent a linear function that is not proportional. The set of even, positive numbers is represented by a function with a y-intercept of 0. The set of odd, positive numbers is represented by a function with a y-intercept of 1.

SET OPERATIONS WITH VENN DIAGRAMS

A Venn diagram is a useful visual tool for representing two or three sets and their common elements. Each set is drawn as a **circle**, with the different circles overlapping. Elements are placed in the circle corresponding to the appropriate set or sets—or placed outside all the circles if they belong to the universe of discourse but not to any of the sets.

For example, suppose our universe of discourse is the integers from 1 to 9, and we have the three sets $A = \{1, 2, 3, 4, 5, 6\}$, $B = \{4, 5, 6, 7\}$, and $C = \{3, 6, 9\}$. This could be illustrated with the following **Venn diagram**:

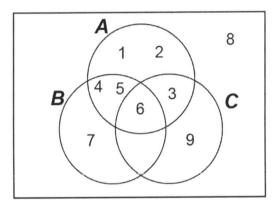

Note, for example, that 6 appears in the center of the diagram where all three circles overlap, because it is an element of all three sets. On the other hand, 8 is placed outside the three circles because it is not an element of any of the sets. Sometimes, instead of writing the elements themselves in the diagram, the total *number* of elements in each part of the Venn diagram is noted. This is especially useful for solving problems involving these numbers of elements.

USING VENN DIAGRAMS TO SOLVE PROBLEMS

Venn diagrams are useful for solving problems involving the numbers of elements in sets and in their intersections. By putting those numbers into a Venn diagram, it's simple to see how many must be in the "leftover" parts.

For example, suppose we're told that 200 voters were polled about two propositions, Proposition 1 and Proposition 2. Further,120 support Proposition 1, 85 support Proposition 2, and 50 support both propositions. To find how many of the voters support neither proposition, we can draw a Venn diagram with a circle representing the supporters of each proposition. We know 50 voters support both propositions, so we can write a 50 in the center of the diagram.

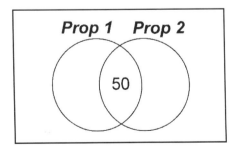

The Proposition 1 circle should contain 120 voters total, so subtracting the 50 voters in the overlap, the other section of the circle must contain 120 − 50 = 70. Similarly, the nonoverlapping part of the Proposition 2 circle should contain 85 − 50 = 35.

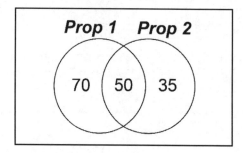

Adding all three sections, the total number of voters supporting either proposition is 70 + 50 + 35 = 155, so there must be 200 − 155 = 45 voters who support neither.

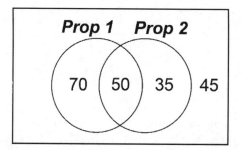

PROPERTIES OF INFINITE SETS

An infinite set has an infinite number of elements. a more technical definition is that a set is **infinite** if its elements can be put in one-to-one correspondence with the elements of one of its proper subsets. For instance, consider the set of all positive integers, $\mathbb{Z}^+$. If we remove the number 1, we can still match up every positive integer to an element of the remaining subset (by simply matching the number n to the number $n + 1$). $\mathbb{Z}^+$ is therefore an infinite set.

The union of an infinite set and any other set is always infinite. the intersection of two infinite sets may or may not be infinite. For instance, consider the set P of prime numbers, the set O of positive odd integers, and the set E of positive even integers—all infinite sets. $P \cap O$ is another infinite set, because there are infinitely many odd prime numbers. $P \cap E$ is finite, because there is only one even prime number. and $E \cap O$ is the empty set. Likewise, the complement of an infinite set may be infinite, finite, or the empty set (if the set equals the universe of discourse).

CARDINALITY

Although all infinite sets have infinitely many members, they may still have different sizes. Two sets are defined to have the same size—or more technically the same **cardinality**—if each element of one set can be matched up to a unique element of the other, with none left over. For example, the set of all integers, $\mathbb{Z}$, and the set of all *even* integers have the same cardinality, even though the latter is a proper subset of the former: every number n in $\mathbb{Z}$ can be matched to a unique number $2n$ in the set of all *even* integers. Although it's more difficult to prove, the set of all rational numbers, $\mathbb{Q}$, also has the same cardinality as $\mathbb{Z}$. However, the set of all real numbers, $\mathbb{R}$, does *not* have the same cardinality—it is impossible to match each integer to a unique real number without any real numbers left over. The most famous proof of this fact was developed by Georg Cantor, and is called the *diagonal argument*.

Sets with the same cardinality as $\mathbb{Z}$ are said to be "countably infinite," or simply **countable**. Sets with a larger cardinality are said to be "uncountably infinite," or **uncountable**.

CARTESIAN PRODUCTS/RELATIONS

A Cartesian product is the product of two sets of data, X and Y, such that all elements x are a member of set X, and all elements y are a member of set Y. The product of the two sets, $X \times Y$ is the set of all ordered pairs (x, y). For example, given a standard deck of 52 playing cards, there are four possible suits (hearts, diamonds, clubs, and spades) and thirteen possible card values (the numbers 2 through 10, ace, jack, queen, and king). If the card suits are set X and the card values are set Y, then there are $4 \times 13 = 52$ possible different (x, y) combinations, as seen in the 52 cards of a standard deck.

A binary relation, also referred to as a relation, dyadic relation, or 2-place relation, is a subset of a Cartesian product. It shows the relation between one set of objects and a second set of objects, or between one set of objects and itself. The prefix *bi-* means *two*, so there are always two sets involved—either two different sets, or the same set used twice. The ordered pairs of the Cartesian product are used to indicate a binary relation. Relations are possible for situations involving more than two sets, but those are not called binary relations.

The five types of relations are reflexive, symmetric, transitive, antisymmetric, and equivalence. A reflexive relation has $x\Re x$ (x related to x) for all values of x in the set. A symmetric relation has $x\Re y \Rightarrow y\Re x$ for all values of x and y in the set. A transitive relation has $(x\Re y$ and $y\Re z) \Rightarrow x\Re z$ for all values of x, y, and z in the set. An antisymmetric relation has $(x\Re y$ and $y\Re x) \Rightarrow x = y$ for all values of x and y in the set. A relation that is reflexive, symmetric, and transitive is called an equivalence relation.

VERTEX-EDGE GRAPHS

A **vertex-edge graph** is a set of items or objects connected by pathways or links. As an example, consider the following set of nodes and a few graphs representing ways of connecting them with edges.

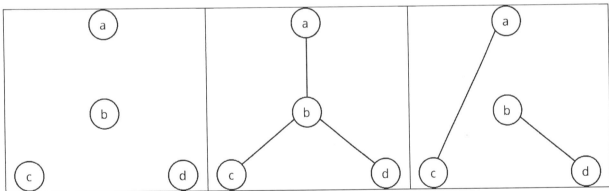

Vertex-edge graphs are useful for solving problems involving schedules, relationships, networks, or paths among a set number of objects. The number of objects may be large, but it will never be infinite. The **vertices** or points on the graph represent the objects and may also be referred to as **nodes**. The nodes are joined by line segments called **edges** or links that show the specific paths that connect the various elements represented by the nodes. The number of nodes does not have to equal the number of edges. There may be more or less, depending on the number of allowable paths.

31

Copyright © Mometrix Media. You have been licensed one copy of this document for personal use only. Any other reproduction or redistribution is strictly prohibited. All rights reserved. This content is provided for test preparation purposes only and does not imply an endorsement by Mometrix of any particular political, scientific, or religious point of view.

An **endpoint** on a vertex-edge graph is a vertex on exactly one edge. In the case of a vertex that is an endpoint, the edge that the vertex is on is incident with the vertex. Two edges are considered to be adjacent if they share a vertex. Two vertices are considered to be adjacent if they share an edge.

In a vertex-edge graph, a **loop** is an edge that has the same vertex as both endpoints. To calculate the **degree of a vertex** in a vertex-edge graph, count the number of edges that are incident with the vertex, counting loops twice since they meet the vertex at both ends. The **degree sum formula** states that the sum of the degrees of all vertices on a vertex-edge graph is always equal to twice the number of edges on the graph. Thus, the sum of the degrees will never be odd, even if there are an odd number of vertices. Consider the following graph. Node d is an endpoint, there is a loop on node b, and the degree sum of the graph is $2 \times 5 = 10$.

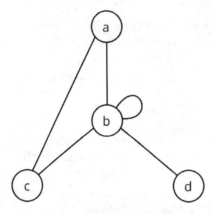

In a vertex-edge graph, a **path** is a given sequence of vertices that follows one or more edges to get from vertex to vertex. There is no jumping over spaces to get from one vertex to the next, although doubling back over an edge already traveled is allowed. A **simple path** is a path that does not repeat an edge in traveling from beginning to end. Think of the vertex-edge graph as a map, with the vertices as cities on the map, and the edges as roads between the cities. To get from one city to another, you must drive on the roads. A simple path allows you to complete your trip without driving on the same road twice.

In a vertex-edge graph, a **circuit** is a path that has the same starting and stopping point. Picturing the vertex-edge graph as a map with cities and roads, a circuit is like leaving home on vacation and then returning home after you have visited your intended destinations. You may go in one direction and then turn around, or you may go in a circle. A **simple circuit** on the graph completes the circuit

32

without repeating an edge. This is like going on vacation and returning home without driving on the same road twice.

Graph   **Example Paths**

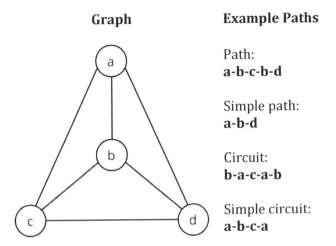

Path:
a-b-c-b-d

Simple path:
a-b-d

Circuit:
b-a-c-a-b

Simple circuit:
a-b-c-a

On a vertex-edge graph, any path that uses each edge exactly one time is called an **Euler path**. One simple way to rule out the possibility of an Euler path is to calculate the degree of each vertex. If more than two vertices have an odd degree, an Euler path is impossible. A path that uses each vertex exactly one time is called a **Hamiltonian path**.

Graph   **Example Paths**

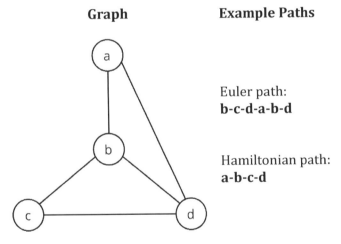

Euler path:
b-c-d-a-b-d

Hamiltonian path:
a-b-c-d

If every pair of vertices is joined by an edge, the vertex-edge graph is said to be **complete**. If the vertex-edge graph has no simple circuits in it, then the graph is said to be a **tree**. If every vertex is connected to every other vertex by some *path*, then the graph is said to be **connected**, otherwise it is **disconnected**.

Complete and Connected **Tree and Connected** **Disconnected**

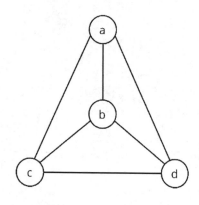 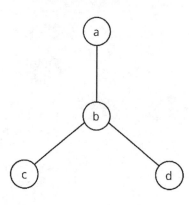 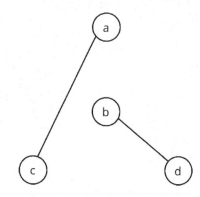

PRACTICE

P1. Given the sets $X = \{1, 2, 3, 4, 5\}$, $Y = \{2, 4, 6, 8\}$, and $Z = \{1, 3, 7, 13, 21\}$ find the following:

(a) $X \cup Y$

(b) $X \cap Y$

(c) $X \cup (Y \cap Z)$

(d) $(X \cup Y) \cap Z$

P2. Give the most precise description of the following paths for the vertex-edge graph:

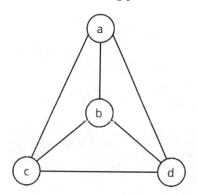

(a) a-d-c

(b) b-d-b-d-b

(c) b-c-d-a-b-d

(d) b-c-d-a

(e) b-c-d-a-b

PRACTICE SOLUTIONS

P1. (a) The union operation includes all elements of the sets being operated on. Thus:

$$X \cup Y = \{1, 2, 3, 4, 5, 6, 8\}$$

(b) The intersection operation includes only elements in both sets being operated on. Thus:

$$X \cap Y = \{2, 4\}$$

(c) First, find the intersection of Y and Z:

$$Y \cap Z = \{\emptyset\}$$

Then, since the intersection of Y and Z is the null set, the union with X is just the elements of X:

$$X \cup (Y \cap Z) = \{1, 2, 3, 4, 5\}$$

(d) First, find the union of X and Y:

$$X \cup Y = \{1, 2, 3, 4, 5, 6, 8\}$$

Then, the intersection of $X \cup Y$ with Z is:

$$(X \cup Y) \cap Z = \{1, 3\}$$

P2. Determine the start and end vertices, whether the path uses all vertices or edges, and whether the path repeats any vertices or edges:

	Same Start and End	Uses All Vertices	Uses All Edges	Repeats Vertices	Repeats Edges	Result
(a)	No	No	No	No	No	Simple Path
(b)	Yes	No	No	Yes	Yes	Circuit
(c)	No	Yes	No	Yes	No	Path
(d)	No	Yes	No	No	No	Hamiltonian Path
(e)	Yes	Yes	No	Yes	No	Simple Circuit

Trigonometry and Calculus

Trigonometry

DEGREES, RADIANS, AND THE UNIT CIRCLE

It is important to understand the deep connection between trigonometry and circles. Specifically, the two main units, **degrees** (°) and **radians** (rad), that are used to measure angles are related this way: 360° in one full circle and 2π radians in one full circle: (360° = 2π rad). The conversion factor relating the two is often stated as $\frac{180°}{\pi}$. For example, to convert $\frac{3\pi}{2}$ radians to degrees, multiply by the conversion factor: $\frac{3\pi}{2} \times \frac{180°}{\pi} = 270°$. As another example, to convert 60° to radians, divide by the conversion factor or multiply by the reciprocal: $60° \times \frac{\pi}{180°} = \frac{\pi}{3}$ radians.

Recall that the standard equation for a circle is $(x - h)^2 + (y - k)^2 = r^2$. A **unit circle** is a circle with a radius of 1 ($r = 1$) that has its center at the origin ($h = 0, k = 0$). Thus, the equation for the unit circle simplifies from the standard equation down to $x^2 + y^2 = 1$.

Standard position is the position of an angle of measure θ whose vertex is at the origin, the initial side crosses the unit circle at the point $(1, 0)$, and the terminal side crosses the unit circle at some other point (a, b). In the standard position, $\sin \theta = b$, $\cos \theta = a$, and $\tan \theta = \frac{b}{a}$.

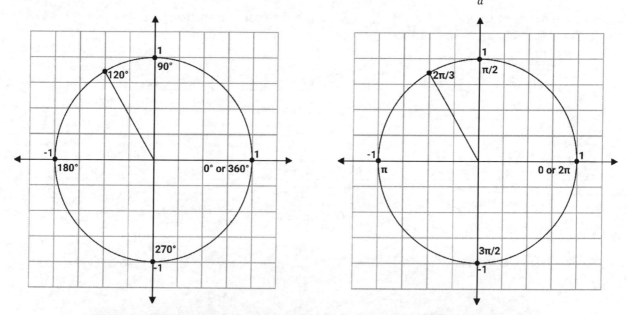

> **Review Video: Unit Circles and Standard Position**
> Visit mometrix.com/academy and enter code: 333922

BASIC TRIGONOMETRIC FUNCTIONS

SINE

The **sine** (sin) function has a period of 360° or 2π radians. This means that its graph makes one complete cycle every 360° or 2π. Because $\sin 0 = 0$, the graph of $y = \sin x$ begins at the origin, with the x-axis representing the angle measure, and the y-axis representing the sine of the angle. The graph of the sine function is a smooth curve that begins at the origin, peaks at the point $\left(\frac{\pi}{2}, 1\right)$, crosses the x-axis at $(\pi, 0)$, has its lowest point at $\left(\frac{3\pi}{2}, -1\right)$, and returns to the x-axis to complete one cycle at $(2\pi, 0)$.

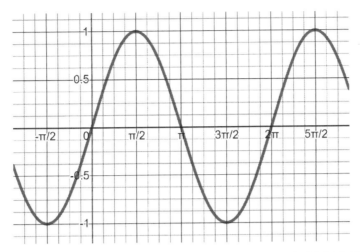

COSINE

The **cosine** (cos) function also has a period of 360° or 2π radians, which means that its graph also makes one complete cycle every 360° or 2π. Because $\cos 0° = 1$, the graph of $y = \cos x$ begins at the point $(0, 1)$, with the x-axis representing the angle measure, and the y-axis representing the cosine of the angle. The graph of the cosine function is a smooth curve that begins at the point $(0, 1)$, crosses the x-axis at the point $\left(\frac{\pi}{2}, 0\right)$, has its lowest point at $(\pi, -1)$, crosses the x-axis again at the point $\left(\frac{3\pi}{2}, 0\right)$, and returns to a peak at the point $(2\pi, 1)$ to complete one cycle.

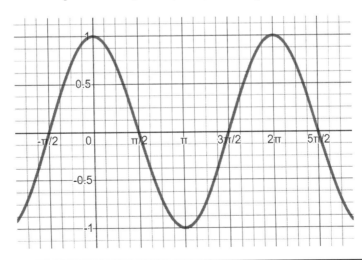

TANGENT

The **tangent** (tan) function has a period of 180° or π radians, which means that its graph makes one complete cycle every 180° or π radians. The x-axis represents the angle measure, and the y-axis represents the tangent of the angle. The graph of the tangent function is a series of smooth curves that cross the x-axis at every 180° or π radians and have an asymptote every $k \times 90°$ or $\frac{k\pi}{2}$ radians, where k is an odd integer. This can be explained by the fact that the tangent is calculated by dividing the sine by the cosine, since the cosine equals zero at those asymptote points.

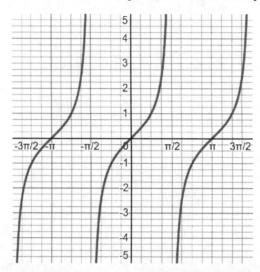

DEFINED AND RECIPROCAL FUNCTIONS

The tangent function is defined as the ratio of the sine to the cosine: $\tan x = \frac{\sin x}{\cos x}$.

To take the reciprocal of a number means to place that number as the denominator of a fraction with a numerator of 1. The reciprocal functions are thus defined quite simply.

Cosecant	$\csc x$	$\dfrac{1}{\sin x}$
Secant	$\sec x$	$\dfrac{1}{\cos x}$
Cotangent	$\cot x$	$\dfrac{1}{\tan x}$

It is important to know these reciprocal functions, but they are not as commonly used as the three basic functions.

INVERSE FUNCTIONS

Each of the trigonometric functions accepts an angular measure, either degrees or radians, and gives a numerical value as the output. The inverse functions do the opposite; they accept a numerical value and give an angular measure as the output.

The inverse of sine, or arcsine, commonly written as either $\sin^{-1} x$ or arcsin x, gives the angle whose sine is x. Similarly:

The inverse of $\cos x$ is written as $\cos^{-1} x$ or arccos x and means the angle whose cosine is x.
The inverse of $\tan x$ is written as $\tan^{-1} x$ or arctan x and means the angle whose tangent is x.
The inverse of $\csc x$ is written as $\csc^{-1} x$ or arccsc x and means the angle whose cosecant is x.
The inverse of $\sec x$ is written as $\sec^{-1} x$ or arcsec x and means the angle whose secant is x.
The inverse of $\cot x$ is written as $\cot^{-1} x$ or arccot x and means the angle whose cotangent is x.

> **Review Video: Inverse Trig Functions**
> Visit mometrix.com/academy and enter code: 156054

IMPORTANT NOTE ABOUT SOLVING TRIGONOMETRIC EQUATIONS

Trigonometric and algebraic equations are solved following the same rules, but while algebraic expressions have one unique solution, trigonometric equations could have multiple solutions, and you must find them all. When solving for an angle with a known trigonometric value, you must consider the sign and include all angles with that value. Your calculator will probably only give one value as an answer, typically in the following ranges:

- For $\sin^{-1} x$, $\left[-\frac{\pi}{2}, \frac{\pi}{2}\right]$ or $[-90°, 90°]$
- For $\cos^{-1} x$, $[0, \pi]$ or $[0°, 180°]$
- For $\tan^{-1} x$, $\left[-\frac{\pi}{2}, \frac{\pi}{2}\right]$ or $[-90°, 90°]$

It is important to determine if there is another angle in a different quadrant that also satisfies the problem. To do this, find the other quadrant(s) with the same sign for that trigonometric function and find the angle that has the same reference angle. Then check whether this angle is also a solution.

- In the first quadrant, all six trigonometric functions are positive.
- In the second quadrant, sin and csc are positive.
- In the third quadrant, tan and cot are positive.
- In the fourth quadrant, cos and sec are positive.

If you remember the phrase, "ALL Students Take Classes," you will be able to remember the sign of each trigonometric function in each quadrant. ALL represents all the signs in the first quadrant. The "S" in "Students" represents the sine function and its reciprocal in the second quadrant. The "T" in "Take" represents the tangent function and its reciprocal in the third quadrant. The "C" in "Classes" represents the cosine function and its reciprocal.

DOMAIN, RANGE, AND ASYMPTOTES IN TRIGONOMETRY

The domain is the set of all possible real number values of x on the graph of a trigonometric function. Some graphs will impose limits on the values of x.

The range is the set of all possible real number values of y on the graph of a trigonometric function. Some graphs will impose limits on the values of y.

Asymptotes are lines that the graph of a trigonometric function approaches but never reaches. Asymptotes exist for values of x in the graphs of the tangent, cotangent, secant, and cosecant. The sine and cosine graphs do not have any asymptotes.

DOMAIN, RANGE, AND ASYMPTOTES OF THE SIX TRIGONOMETRIC FUNCTIONS

The domain, range, and asymptotes for each of the trigonometric functions are as follows:

- In the **sine** function, the domain is all real numbers, the range is $-1 \leq y \leq 1$, and there are no asymptotes.

- In the **cosine** function, the domain is all real numbers, the range is $-1 \leq y \leq 1$, and there are no asymptotes.

- In the **tangent** function, the domain is $x \in \mathbb{R}; x \neq \frac{\pi}{2} + k\pi$, the range is all real numbers, and the asymptotes are the lines $x = \frac{\pi}{2} + k\pi$.

- In the **cosecant** function, the domain is $x \in \mathbb{R}; x \neq k\pi$, the range is $(-\infty, -1]$ and $[1, \infty)$, and the asymptotes are the lines $x = k\pi$.

- In the **secant** function, the domain is $x \in \mathbb{R}; x \neq \frac{\pi}{2} + k\pi$, the range is $(-\infty, 1]$ and $[1, \infty)$, and the asymptotes are the lines $x = \frac{\pi}{2} + k\pi$.

- In the **cotangent** function, the domain is $x \in \mathbb{R}; x \neq k\pi$, the range is all real numbers, and the asymptotes are the lines $x = k\pi$.

In each of the above cases, k represents any integer.

TRIGONOMETRIC IDENTITIES
SUM AND DIFFERENCE

To find the sine, cosine, or tangent of the sum or difference of two angles, use one of the following formulas where α and β are two angles with known sine, cosine, or tangent values as needed:

$$\sin(\alpha \pm \beta) = \sin \alpha \cos \beta \pm \cos \alpha \sin \beta$$
$$\cos(\alpha \pm \beta) = \cos \alpha \cos \beta \mp \sin \alpha \sin \beta$$
$$\tan(\alpha \pm \beta) = \frac{\tan \alpha \pm \tan \beta}{1 \mp \tan \alpha \tan \beta}$$

HALF ANGLE

To find the sine or cosine of half of a known angle, use the following formulas where θ is an angle with a known exact cosine value:

$$\sin\left(\frac{\theta}{2}\right) = \pm\sqrt{\frac{(1 - \cos\theta)}{2}}$$

$$\cos\left(\frac{\theta}{2}\right) = \pm\sqrt{\frac{(1 + \cos\theta)}{2}}$$

40

To determine the sign of the answer, you must recognize which quadrant the given angle is in and apply the correct sign for the trigonometric function you are using. If you need to find an expression for the exact sine or cosine of an angle that you do not know, such as sine 22.5°, you can rewrite the given angle as a half angle, such as $\sin\left(\frac{45°}{2}\right)$, and use the formula above:

$$\sin\left(\frac{45°}{2}\right) = \pm\sqrt{\frac{(1-\cos(45°))}{2}} = \pm\sqrt{\frac{\left(1-\frac{\sqrt{2}}{2}\right)}{2}} = \pm\sqrt{\frac{(2-\sqrt{2})}{4}} = \pm\frac{1}{2}\sqrt{(2-\sqrt{2})}$$

To find the tangent or cotangent of half of a known angle, use the following formulas where θ is an angle with known exact sine and cosine values:

$$\tan\frac{\theta}{2} = \frac{\sin\theta}{1+\cos\theta}$$
$$\cot\frac{\theta}{2} = \frac{\sin\theta}{1-\cos\theta}$$

These formulas will work for finding the tangent or cotangent of half of any angle unless the cosine of θ happens to make the denominator of the identity equal to 0.

The Pythagorean theorem states that $a^2 + b^2 = c^2$ for all right triangles. The trigonometric identity that derives from this principle is stated in this way: $\sin^2\theta + \cos^2\theta = 1$.

Dividing each term by either $\sin^2\theta$ or $\cos^2\theta$ yields two other identities, respectively:

$$1 + \cot^2\theta = \csc^2\theta$$
$$\tan^2\theta + 1 = \sec^2\theta$$

DOUBLE ANGLES

In each case, use one of the double angle formulas. To find the sine or cosine of twice a known angle, use one of the following formulas:

$$\sin(2\theta) = 2\sin\theta\cos\theta$$

$$\cos(2\theta) = \cos^2\theta - \sin^2\theta$$
$$= 2\cos^2\theta - 1$$
$$= 1 - 2\sin^2\theta$$

To find the tangent or cotangent of twice a known angle, use the formulas where θ is an angle with known exact sine, cosine, tangent, and cotangent values:

$$\tan(2\theta) = \frac{2\tan\theta}{1-\tan^2\theta}$$
$$\cot(2\theta) = \frac{\cot\theta - \tan\theta}{2}$$

PRODUCTS

To find the product of the sines and cosines of two different angles, use one of the following formulas where α and β are two unique angles:

$$\sin\alpha\sin\beta = \frac{1}{2}[\cos(\alpha-\beta)-\cos(\alpha+\beta)]$$

$$\cos\alpha\cos\beta = \frac{1}{2}[\cos(\alpha+\beta)+\cos(\alpha-\beta)]$$

$$\sin\alpha\cos\beta = \frac{1}{2}[\sin(\alpha+\beta)+\sin(\alpha-\beta)]$$

$$\cos\alpha\sin\beta = \frac{1}{2}[\sin(\alpha+\beta)-\sin(\alpha-\beta)]$$

COMPLEMENTARY

The trigonometric cofunction identities use the trigonometric relationships of complementary angles (angles whose sum is 90°). These are:

$$\cos x = \sin(90°-x)$$
$$\csc x = \sec(90°-x)$$
$$\cot x = \tan(90°-x)$$

TABLE OF COMMONLY ENCOUNTERED ANGLES

$0° = 0$ radians, $30° = \frac{\pi}{6}$ radians, $45° = \frac{\pi}{4}$ radians, $60° = \frac{\pi}{3}$ radians, and $90° = \frac{\pi}{2}$ radians

$\sin 0° = 0$	$\cos 0° = 1$	$\tan 0° = 0$
$\sin 30° = \frac{1}{2}$	$\cos 30° = \frac{\sqrt{3}}{2}$	$\tan 30° = \frac{\sqrt{3}}{3}$
$\sin 45° = \frac{\sqrt{2}}{2}$	$\cos 45° = \frac{\sqrt{2}}{2}$	$\tan 45° = 1$
$\sin 60° = \frac{\sqrt{3}}{2}$	$\cos 60° = \frac{1}{2}$	$\tan 60° = \sqrt{3}$
$\sin 90° = 1$	$\cos 90° = 0$	$\tan 90° = $ undefined
$\csc 0° = $ undefined	$\sec 0° = 1$	$\cot 0° = $ undefined
$\csc 30° = 2$	$\sec 30° = \frac{2\sqrt{3}}{3}$	$\cot 30° = \sqrt{3}$
$\csc 45° = \sqrt{2}$	$\sec 45° = \sqrt{2}$	$\cot 45° = 1$
$\csc 60° = \frac{2\sqrt{3}}{3}$	$\sec 60° = 2$	$\cot 60° = \frac{\sqrt{3}}{3}$
$\csc 90° = 1$	$\sec 90° = $ undefined	$\cot 90° = 0$

The values in the upper half of this table are values you should have memorized or be able to find quickly and those in the lower half can easily be determined as the reciprocal of the corresponding function.

RECTANGULAR AND POLAR COORDINATES

Rectangular coordinates are those that lie on the square grids of the Cartesian plane. They should be quite familiar to you. The polar coordinate system is based on a circular graph, rather than the square grid of the Cartesian system. Points in the polar coordinate system are in the format (r, θ), where r is the distance from the origin (think radius of the circle) and θ is the smallest positive angle (moving counterclockwise around the circle) made with the positive horizontal axis.

To convert a point from rectangular (x, y) format to polar (r, θ) format, use the formula (x, y) to $(r, \theta) \Rightarrow r = \sqrt{x^2 + y^2}$; $\theta = \arctan\frac{y}{x}$ when $x \neq 0$.

If x is positive, use the positive square root value for r. If x is negative, use the negative square root value for r. If $x = 0$, use the following rules:

- If $y = 0$, then $\theta = 0$.
- If $y > 0$, then $\theta = \frac{\pi}{2}$.
- If $y < 0$, then $\theta = \frac{3\pi}{2}$.

To convert a point from polar (r, θ) format to rectangular (x, y) format, use the formula (r, θ) to $(x, y) \Rightarrow x = r \cos \theta$; $y = r \sin \theta$.

DE MOIVRE'S THEOREM

De Moivre's theorem is used to find the powers of complex numbers (numbers that contain the imaginary number i) written in polar form. Given a trigonometric expression that contains i, such as $z = r \cos x + ir \sin x$, where r is a real number and x is an angle measurement in polar form, use the formula $z^n = r^n(\cos nx + i \sin nx)$, where r and n are real numbers, x is the angle measure in polar form, and i is the imaginary number $i = \sqrt{-1}$. The expression $\cos x + i \sin x$ can be written cis x, making the formula appear in the format $z^n = r^n$ cis nx.

Note that De Moivre's theorem is only for angles in polar form. If you are given an angle in degrees, you must convert to polar form before using the formula.

COMPLEX NUMBERS

Complex numbers consist of a real component and an imaginary component. Complex numbers are expressed in the form $a + bi$ with real component a and imaginary component bi. The imaginary unit i is equal to $\sqrt{-1}$. That means $i^2 = -1$. The imaginary unit provides a way to find the square root of a negative number. For example, $\sqrt{-25}$ is $5i$. You should expect questions asking you to add, subtract, multiply, divide, and simplify complex numbers. You may see a question that says, "Add $3 + 2i$ and $5 - 7i$" or "Subtract $4 + i\sqrt{5}$ from $2 + i\sqrt{5}$." Or you may see a question that says, "Multiply $6 + 2i$ by $8 - 4i$" or "Divide $1 - 3i$ by $9 - 7i$."

OPERATIONS ON COMPLEX NUMBERS

Operations with complex numbers resemble operations with variables in algebra. When adding or subtracting complex numbers, you can only combine like terms—real terms with real terms and imaginary terms with imaginary terms. For example, if you are asked to simplify the expression $-2 + 4i - (-3 + 7i) - 5i$, you should first remove the parentheses to yield $-2 + 4i + 3 - 7i - 5i$. Combining like terms yields $1 - 8i$. One interesting aspect of imaginary numbers is that if i has an exponent greater than 1, it can be simplified. Example: $i^2 = -1$, $i^3 = -i$, and $i^4 = 1$. When multiplying complex numbers, remember to simplify each i with an exponent greater than 1. For example, you might see a question that says, "Simplify $(2 - i)(3 + 2i)$." You need to distribute and multiply to get $6 + 4i - 3i - 2i^2$. This is further simplified to $6 + i - 2(-1)$, or $8 + i$.

SIMPLIFYING EXPRESSIONS WITH COMPLEX DENOMINATORS

If an expression contains an i in the denominator, it must be simplified. Remember, roots cannot be left in the denominator of a fraction. Since i is equivalent to $\sqrt{-1}$, i cannot be left in the denominator of a fraction. You must rationalize the denominator of a fraction that contains a complex denominator by multiplying the numerator and denominator by the conjugate of the denominator. The conjugate of the complex number $a + bi$ is $a - bi$. You can simplify $\frac{2}{5i}$ by simply multiplying $\frac{2}{5i} \times \frac{i}{i}$, which yields $-\frac{2}{5}i$. And you can simplify $\frac{5+3i}{2-4i}$ by multiplying $\frac{5+3i}{2-4i} \times \frac{2+4i}{2+4i}$. This yields $\frac{10+20i+6i-12}{4-8i+8i+16}$ which simplifies to $\frac{-2+26i}{20}$ or $\frac{-1+13i}{10}$, which can also be written as $-\frac{1}{10} + \frac{13}{10}i$.

PRACTICE

P1. Convert the following angles from degrees to radians:

   (a) $56°$

   (b) $12°$

   (c) $199°$

P2. Convert the following angles from radians to degrees:

   (a) 3

   (b) 3π

   (c) 33

P3. Simplify the following trigonometric expressions:

   (a) $\frac{\sin x \tan x + \cos x}{\sec x}$

   (b) $\frac{4 \cos 2x}{\sin^2 2x} + \sec^2 x$

PRACTICE SOLUTIONS

P1. Multiply each by the conversion factor $\frac{\pi}{180°}$:

   (a) $56° \times \frac{\pi}{180°} \approx 0.977$

   (b) $12° \times \frac{\pi}{180°} \approx 0.209$

   (c) $199° \times \frac{\pi}{180°} \approx 3.473$

P2. Multiply each by the conversion factor $\frac{180°}{\pi}$:

(a) $3 \times \frac{180°}{\pi} \approx 171.9°$

(b) $3\pi \times \frac{180°}{\pi} = 540° = 180°$

(c) $33 \times \frac{180°}{\pi} \approx 1890.8° \approx 90.8°$

P3. (a) Utilize trigonometric identities and definitions to simplify. Specifically, $\tan x = \frac{\sin x}{\cos x}$, $\sec x = \frac{1}{\cos x}$, and $\sin^2 x + \cos^2 x = 1$:

$$\frac{\sin x \tan x + \cos x}{\sec x} = \left(\sin x \frac{\sin x}{\cos x} + \cos x\right)\cos x$$
$$= \frac{\sin^2 x}{\cos x}\cos x + \cos^2 x$$
$$= \sin^2 x + \cos^2 x$$
$$= 1$$

(b) Utilize trigonometric identities and definitions to simplify. Specifically, double angle formulas, $\sin^2 x = (\sin x)^2$, and $\sin^2 x + \cos^2 x = 1$:

$$\frac{4\cos 2x}{\sin^2 2x} + \sec^2 x = \frac{4(\cos^2 x - \sin^2 x)}{4\sin^2 x \cos^2 x} + \sec^2 x$$
$$= \frac{\cos^2 x - \sin^2 x}{\sin^2 x \cos^2 x} + \sec^2 x$$
$$= \frac{\cos^2 x}{\sin^2 x \cos^2 x} - \frac{\sin^2 x}{\sin^2 x \cos^2 x} + \sec^2 x$$
$$= \frac{1}{\sin^2 x} - \frac{1}{\cos^2 x} + \sec^2 x$$
$$= \csc^2 x - \sec^2 x + \sec^2 x$$
$$= \csc^2 x$$

Calculus

CALCULUS

Calculus, also called analysis, is the branch of mathematics that studies the length, area, and volume of objects, and the rate of change of quantities (which can be expressed as slopes of curves). The two principal branches of calculus are differential and integral. **Differential calculus** is based on derivatives and takes the form,

$$\frac{d}{dx} f(x)$$

Integral calculus is based on integrals and takes the form,

$$\int f(x)dx$$

Some of the basic ideas of calculus were utilized as far back in history as Archimedes. However, its modern forms were developed by Newton and Leibniz.

LIMITS

The **limit of a function** is represented by the notation $\lim_{x \to a} f(x)$. It is read as "the limit of f of x as x approaches a." In many cases, $\lim_{x \to a} f(x)$ will simply be equal to $f(a)$, but not always. Limits are important because some functions are not defined or are not easy to evaluate at certain values of x.

The limit at the point is said to exist only if the limit is the same when approached from the right side as from the left: $\lim_{x \to a^+} f(x) = \lim_{x \to a^-} f(x)$). Notice the symbol by the a in each case. When x approaches a from the right, it approaches from the positive end of the number line. When x approaches a from the left, it approaches from the negative end of the number line.

If the limit as x approaches a differs depending on the direction from which it approaches, then the limit does not exist at a. In other words, if $\lim_{x \to a^+} f(x)$ does not equal $\lim_{x \to a^-} f(x)$, then the limit does not exist at a. The limit also does not exist if either of the one-sided limits does not exist.

Situations in which the limit does not exist include a function that jumps from one value to another at a, one that oscillates between two different values as x approaches a, or one that increases or decreases without bounds as x approaches a. If the limit you calculate has a value of $\frac{c}{0}$, where c is any constant, this means the function goes to infinity and the limit does not exist.

It is possible for two functions that do not have limits to be multiplied to get a new function that does have a limit. Just because two functions do not have limits, do not assume that the product will not have a limit.

DIRECT SUBSTITUTION

The first thing to try when looking for a limit is direct substitution. To find the limit of a function $\lim_{x \to a} f(x)$ by direct substitution, substitute the value of a for x in the function and solve. The following patterns apply to finding the limit of a function by direct substitution:

$$\lim_{x \to a} b = b, \text{ where } b \text{ is any real number}$$

$$\lim_{x \to a} x = a$$

$$\lim_{x \to a} x^n = a^n, \text{ where } n \text{ is any positive integer}$$

$$\lim_{x \to a} \sqrt{x} = \sqrt{a}; a > 0$$

$$\lim_{x \to a} \sqrt[n]{x} = \sqrt[n]{a}, \text{ where } n \text{ is a positive integer and } a > 0 \text{ for all even values of } n$$

$$\lim_{x \to a} \frac{1}{x} = \frac{1}{a}; a \neq 0$$

You can also use substitution for finding the limit of a trigonometric function, a polynomial function, or a rational function. Be sure that in manipulating an expression to find a limit that you do not divide by terms equal to zero.

In finding the limit of a composite function, begin by finding the limit of the innermost function. For example, to find $\lim_{x \to a} f(g(x))$, first find the value of $\lim_{x \to a} g(x)$. Then substitute this value for x in $f(x)$ and solve. The result is the limit of the original problem.

LIMITS AND OPERATIONS

When finding the limit of the sum or difference of two functions, find the limit of each individual function and then add or subtract the results. Example:

$$\lim_{x \to a}[f(x) \pm g(x)] = \lim_{x \to a} f(x) \pm \lim_{x \to a} g(x)$$

To find the limit of the product or quotient of two functions, find the limit of each individual function and then multiply or divide the results. Example:

$$\lim_{x \to a}[f(x) \times g(x)] = \lim_{x \to a} f(x) \times \lim_{x \to a} g(x)$$

$$\lim_{x \to a} \frac{f(x)}{g(x)} = \frac{\lim_{x \to a} f(x)}{\lim_{x \to a} g(x)}, \text{ where } g(x) \neq 0$$

$$\lim_{x \to a} g(x) \neq 0$$

When finding the quotient of the limits of two functions, make sure the denominator is not equal to zero. If it is, use differentiation or L'Hôpital's rule to find the limit.

To find the limit of a power of a function or a root of a function, find the limit of the function and then raise the limit to the original power or take the root of the limit. Example:

$$\lim_{x \to a} [f(x)]^n = \left[\lim_{x \to a} f(x) \right]^n$$

$$\lim_{x \to a} \sqrt[n]{f(x)} = \sqrt[n]{\lim_{x \to a} f(x)}, \text{ where } n \text{ is a positive integer}$$

$$\lim_{x \to a} f(x) > 0 \text{ for all even values of } n$$

To find the limit of a function multiplied by a scalar, find the limit of the function and multiply the result by the scalar. Example:

$$\lim_{x \to a} kf(x) = k \lim_{x \to a} f(x), \text{ where } k \text{ is a real number.}$$

L'HÔPITAL'S RULE

Sometimes solving $\lim_{x \to a} \frac{f(x)}{g(x)}$ by the direct substitution method will result in the numerator and denominator both being equal to zero, or both being equal to infinity. This outcome is called an indeterminate form. The limit cannot be directly found by substitution in these cases. L'Hôpital's rule is a useful method for finding the limit of a problem in the indeterminate form. L'Hôpital's rule allows you to find the limit using derivatives. Assuming both the numerator and denominator are differentiable, and that both are equal to zero when the direct substitution method is used, take the derivative of both the numerator and the denominator and then use the direct substitution method. For example, if $\lim_{x \to a} \frac{f(x)}{g(x)} = \frac{0}{0}$, take the derivatives of $f(x)$ and $g(x)$ and then find $\lim_{x \to a} \frac{f'(x)}{g'(x)}$. If $g'(x) \neq 0$, then you have found the limit of the original function. If $g'(x) = 0$ and $f'(x) = 0$, L'Hôpital's rule may be applied to the function $\frac{f'(x)}{g'(x)}$, and so on until either a limit is found, or it can be determined that the limit does not exist.

SQUEEZE THEOREM

The squeeze theorem is known by many names, including the sandwich theorem, the sandwich rule, the squeeze lemma, the squeezing theorem, and the pinching theorem. No matter what you call it, the principle is the same. To prove the limit of a difficult function exists, find the limits of two functions, one on either side of the unknown, that are easy to compute. If the limits of these functions are equal, then that is also the limit of the unknown function. In mathematical terms, the theorem is:

If $g(x) \leq f(x) \leq h(x)$ for all values of x where $f(x)$ is the function with the unknown limit, and if $\lim_{x \to a} g(x) = \lim_{x \to a} h(x)$, then this limit is also equal to $\lim_{x \to a} f(x)$.

To find the limit of an expression containing an absolute value sign, take the absolute value of the limit. If $\lim_{n \to \infty} a_n = L$, where L is the numerical value for the limit, then $\lim_{n \to \infty} |a_n| = |L|$. Also, if $\lim_{n \to \infty} |a_n| = 0$, then $\lim_{n \to \infty} a_n = 0$. The trick comes when you are asked to find the limit as n

approaches from the left. Whenever the limit is being approached from the left, it is being approached from the negative end of the domain. The absolute value sign makes everything in the equation positive, essentially eliminating the negative side of the domain. In this case, rewrite the equation without the absolute value signs and add a negative sign in front of the expression. Example:

$$\lim_{n \to 0^-} |x| \text{ becomes } \lim_{n \to 0^-} (-x)$$

> **Review Video: Squeeze Theorem**
> Visit mometrix.com/academy and enter code: 383104

DERIVATIVES

The derivative of a function is a measure of how much that function is changing at a specific point, and is the slope of a line tangent to a curve at the specific point. The derivative of a function $f(x)$ is written $f'(x)$, and read, "f prime of x." Other notations for the derivative include $D_x f(x)$, y', $D_x y$, $\frac{dy}{dx}$, and $\frac{d}{dx} f(x)$. The definition of the derivative of a function is $f'(x) = \lim_{h \to 0} \frac{f(x+h) - f(x)}{h}$. However, this formula is rarely used.

There is a simpler method you can use to find the derivative of a polynomial. Given a function $f(x) = a_n x^n + a_{n-1} x^{n-1} + a_{n-2} x^{n-2} + \cdots + a_1 x + a_0$, multiply each exponent by its corresponding coefficient to get the new coefficient and reduce the value of the exponent by one. Coefficients with no variable are dropped. This gives $f'(x) = n a_n x^{n-1} + (n-1) a_{n-1} x^{n-2} + \cdots + a_1$, a pattern that can be repeated for each successive derivative.

Differentiable functions are functions that have a derivative. Some basic rules for finding derivatives of functions are:

$$f(x) = c \Rightarrow f'(x) = 0; \text{ where } c \text{ is a constant}$$
$$f(x) = x \Rightarrow f'(x) = 1$$
$$f(x) = x^n \Rightarrow f'(x) = nx^{n-1}; \text{ where } n \text{ is a real number}$$

$$(cf(x))' = cf'(x); \text{ where } c \text{ is a constant}$$
$$(f + g)'(x) = f'(x) + g'(x)$$
$$(fg)'(x) = f(x)g'(x) + f'(x)g(x)$$
$$\left(\frac{f}{g}\right)'(x) = \frac{f'(x)g(x) - f(x)g'(x)}{[g(x)]^2}$$
$$(f \circ g)'(x) = f'(g(x)) \times g'(x)$$

This last formula is also known as the **chain rule**. If you are finding the derivative of a polynomial that is raised to a power, let the polynomial be represented by $g(x)$ and use the chain rule. The

49

chain rule is one of the most important concepts to grasp in the early stages of learning calculus. Many other rules and shortcuts are based upon the chain rule.

DIFFERENCE QUOTIENT AND DERIVATIVE

A secant is a line that connects two points on a curve. The **difference quotient** gives the slope of an arbitrary secant line that connects the point $(x, f(x))$ with a nearby point $(x + h, f(x + h))$ on the graph of the function f. The difference quotient is the same formula that is always used to determine a slope—the change in y divided by the change in x. It is written as $\frac{f(x+h)-f(x)}{h}$.

A tangent is a line that touches a curve at one point. The tangent and the curve have the same slope at the point where they touch. The derivative is the function that gives the slope of both the tangent and the curve of the function at that point. The derivative is written as the limit of the difference quotient, or:

$$\lim_{h \to 0} \frac{f(x + h) - f(x)}{h}$$

If the function is f, the derivative is denoted as $f'(x)$, and it is the slope of the function f at point $(x, f(x))$. It is expressed as:

$$f'(x) = \lim_{h \to 0} \frac{f(x + h) - f(x)}{h}$$

IMPLICIT FUNCTIONS

An **implicit function** is one where it is impossible, or very difficult, to express one variable in terms of another by normal algebraic methods. This would include functions that have both variables raised to a power greater than 1, functions that have two variables multiplied by each other, or a combination of the two. To differentiate such a function with respect to x, take the derivative of each term that contains a variable, either x or y. When differentiating a term with y, use the chain rule, first taking the derivative with respect to y, and then multiplying by $\frac{dy}{dx}$. If a term contains both

x and y, you will have to use the product rule as well as the chain rule. Once the derivative of each individual term has been found, use the rules of algebra to solve for $\frac{dy}{dx}$ to get the final answer.

Review Video: Implicit Differentiation - Explicitly Explained
Visit mometrix.com/academy and enter code: 102151

DERIVATIVES OF TRIGONOMETRIC FUNCTIONS

Trigonometric functions are any functions that include one of the six trigonometric expressions. The following rules for derivatives apply for all trigonometric differentiation:

$$\frac{d}{dx}(\sin x) = \cos x, \qquad \frac{d}{dx}(\cos x) = -\sin x, \qquad \frac{d}{dx}(\tan x) = \sec^2 x$$

For functions that are a combination of trigonometric and algebraic expressions, use the chain rule:

$$\frac{d}{dx}(\sin u) = \cos u \frac{du}{dx} \qquad \frac{d}{dx}(\sec u) = \tan u \sec u \frac{du}{dx}$$
$$\frac{d}{dx}(\cos u) = -\sin u \frac{du}{dx} \qquad \frac{d}{dx}(\csc u) = -\csc u \cot u \frac{du}{dx}$$
$$\frac{d}{dx}(\tan u) = \sec^2 u \frac{du}{dx} \qquad \frac{d}{dx}(\cot u) = -\csc^2 u \frac{du}{dx}$$

Functions involving the inverses of the trigonometric functions can also be differentiated.

$$\frac{d}{dx}(\sin^{-1} u) = \frac{1}{\sqrt{1-u^2}}\frac{du}{dx} \qquad \frac{d}{dx}(\csc^{-1} u) = \frac{-1}{|u|\sqrt{u^2-1}}\frac{du}{dx}$$
$$\frac{d}{dx}(\cos^{-1} u) = \frac{-1}{\sqrt{1-u^2}}\frac{du}{dx} \qquad \frac{d}{dx}(\sec^{-1} u) = \frac{1}{|u|\sqrt{u^2-1}}\frac{du}{dx}$$
$$\frac{d}{dx}(\tan^{-1} u) = \frac{1}{1+u^2}\frac{du}{dx} \qquad \frac{d}{dx}(\cot^{-1} u) = \frac{-1}{1+u^2}\frac{du}{dx}$$

In each of the above expressions, u represents a differentiable function. Also, the value of u must be such that the radicand, if applicable, is a positive number. Remember the expression $\frac{du}{dx}$ means to take the derivative of the function u with respect to the variable x.

Review Video: Derivatives of Trigonometry Functions
Visit mometrix.com/academy and enter code: 132724

DERIVATIVES OF EXPONENTIAL AND LOGARITHMIC FUNCTIONS

Exponential functions are in the form e^x, which has itself as its derivative: $\frac{d}{dx}e^x = e^x$. For functions that have a function as the exponent rather than just an x, use the formula $\frac{d}{dx}e^u = e^u\frac{du}{dx}$. The inverse of the exponential function is the natural logarithm. To find the derivative of the natural logarithm, use the formula $\frac{d}{dx}\ln u = \frac{1}{u}\frac{du}{dx}$.

If you are trying to solve an expression with a variable in the exponent, use the formula $a^x = e^{x \ln a}$, where a is a positive real number and x is any real number. To find the derivative of a function in this format, use the formula $\frac{d}{dx}a^x = a^x \ln a$. If the exponent is a function rather than a single variable x, use the formula $\frac{d}{dx}a^u = a^u \ln a \frac{du}{dx}$. If you are trying to solve an expression involving a logarithm, use the formula $\frac{d}{dx}(\log_a x) = \frac{1}{x \ln a}$ or $\frac{d}{dx}(\log_a |u|) = \frac{1}{u \ln a}\frac{du}{dx}$; $u \neq 0$.

CONTINUITY

A function can be either continuous or discontinuous. A conceptual way to describe continuity is this: A function is continuous if its graph can be traced with a pen without lifting the pen from the page. In other words, there are no breaks or gaps in the graph of the function. However, this is only a description, not a technical definition. A function is continuous at the point $x = a$ if the three following conditions are met:

1. $f(a)$ is defined
2. $\lim\limits_{x \to a} f(x)$ exists
3. $\lim\limits_{x \to a} f(x) = f(a)$

If any of these conditions are not met, the function is discontinuous at the point $x = a$.

A function can be continuous at a point, continuous over an interval, or continuous everywhere. The above rules define continuity at a point. A function that is continuous over an interval $[a, b]$ is continuous at the points a and b and at every point between them. A function that is continuous everywhere is continuous for every real number, that is, for all points in its domain.

DISCONTINUITY

Discontinuous functions are categorized according to the type or cause of discontinuity. Three examples are point, infinite, and jump discontinuity. A function with a point discontinuity has one value of x for which it is not continuous. A function with infinite discontinuity has a vertical asymptote at $x = a$ and $f(a)$ is undefined. It is said to have an infinite discontinuity at $x = a$. A function with jump discontinuity has one-sided limits from the left and from the right, but they are not equal to one another, that is, $\lim\limits_{x \to a^-} f(x) \neq \lim\limits_{x \to a^+} f(x)$. It is said to have a jump discontinuity at $x = a$.

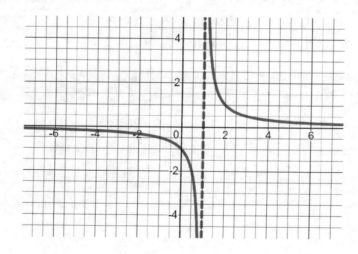

The function, $f(x) = \frac{1}{x-1}$, plotted in the graph has an infinite discontinuity. It has a vertical asymptote at $x = 1$, as such, the function is undefined at $x = 1$.

DIFFERENTIABILITY

A function is said to be differentiable at point $x = a$ if it has a derivative at that point, that is, if $f'(a)$ exists. For a function to be differentiable, it must be continuous because the slope cannot be defined at a point of discontinuity. Furthermore, for a function to be differentiable, its graph must not have any sharp turn for which it is impossible to draw a tangent line. The sine function is an example of a differentiable function. It is continuous, and a tangent line can be drawn anywhere along its graph.

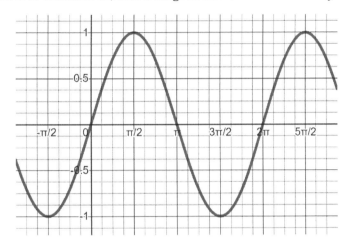

The absolute value function, $f(x) = |x|$, is an example of a function that is not differentiable:

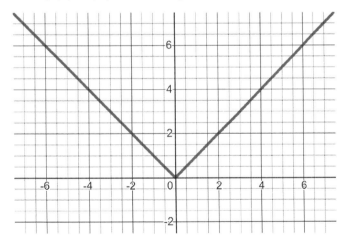

It is continuous, but it has a sharp turn at $x = 0$ which prohibits the drawing of a tangent at that point. All differentiable functions are continuous, but not all continuous functions are differentiable, as the absolute value function demonstrates.

The function $f(x) = \frac{1}{x-1}$ is not differentiable because it is not continuous. It has a discontinuity at $x = 1$. Therefore, a tangent could not be drawn at that point.

APPROXIMATING A DERIVATIVE FROM A TABLE OF VALUES

The derivative of a function at a particular point is equal to the slope of the graph of the function at that point. For a nonlinear function, it can be thought of as the limit of the slope of a line drawn between two other points on the function as those points become closer to the point in question. Such a line drawn through two points on the function is called a **secant** of the function.

This definition of the derivative in terms of the secant allows us to approximate the derivative of a function at a point from a table of values: we take the slope of the line through the points on either side. That is, if the point lies between (x_1, y_1) and (x_2, y_2), the slope of the secant—the approximate derivative—is $\frac{y_2-y_1}{x_2-x_1}$. (This is also equal to the average slope over the interval $[x_1, x_2]$.)

For example, consider the function represented by the following table:

x	0	2	4	6	8	10
y	1	5	8	9	7	4

Suppose we want to know the derivative of the function when $x = 3$. This lies between the points $(2, 5)$ and $(4, 8)$; the approximate derivative is $\frac{8-5}{4-2} = \frac{3}{2}$.

POSITION, VELOCITY, AND ACCELERATION

Velocity is a specific type of rate of change. It refers to the rate of change of the position of an object with relation to a reference frame. **Acceleration** is the rate of change of velocity.

Average velocity over a period of time is found using the formula $\bar{v} = \frac{s(t_2)-s(t_1)}{t_2-t_1}$, where t_1 and t_2 are specific points in time and $s(t_1)$ and $s(t_2)$ are the distances traveled at those points in time.

Instantaneous velocity at a specific time, t, is found using the limit $v = \lim_{h \to 0} \frac{s(t+h)-s(t)}{h}$, or $v = s'(t)$.

Remember that velocity at a given point is found using the first derivative, and acceleration at a given point is found using the second derivative. Therefore, the formula for acceleration at a given point in time is found using the formula $a(t) = v'(t) = s''(t)$, where a is acceleration, v is velocity, and s is displacement.

USING FIRST AND SECOND DERIVATIVES

The **first derivative** of a function is equal to the **rate of change** of the function. The sign of the rate of change shows whether the value of the function is **increasing** or **decreasing**. A positive rate of change—and therefore a positive first derivative—represents that the function is increasing at that point. A negative rate of change represents that the function is decreasing. If the rate of change is zero, the function is not changing, i.e., it is constant.

For example, consider the function $f(x) = x^3 - 6x^2 - 15x + 12$. The derivative of this function is $f'(x) = 3x^2 - 12x - 15 = 3(x^2 - 4x - 5) = 3(x - 5)(x + 1)$. This derivative is a quadratic function with zeroes at $x = 5$ and $x = -1$; by plugging in points in each interval we can find that $f'(x)$ is positive when $x < -1$ and when $x > 5$ and negative when $-1 < x < 5$. Thus $f(x)$ is increasing in the interval $(-\infty, -1) \cup (5, \infty)$ and decreasing in the interval $(-1, 5)$.

EXTREMA

The **maximum** and **minimum** values of a function are collectively called the **extrema** of the function. Both maxima and minima can be local, also known as relative, or absolute. A local maximum or minimum refers to the value of a function near a certain value of x. An absolute maximum or minimum refers to the value of a function on a given interval.

The local maximum of a function is the largest value that the function attains near a certain value of x. For example, function f has a local maximum at $x = b$ if $f(b)$ is the largest value that f attains as it approaches b.

Conversely, the local minimum is the smallest value that the function attains near a certain value of x. In other words, function f has a local minimum at $x = b$ if $f(b)$ is the smallest value that f attains as it approaches b.

The absolute maximum of a function is the largest value of the function over a certain interval. The function f has an absolute maximum at $x = b$ if $f(b) \geq f(x)$ for all x in the domain of f.

The absolute minimum of a function is the smallest value of the function over a certain interval. The function f has an absolute minimum at $x = b$ if $f(b) \leq f(x)$ for all x in the domain of f.

CRITICAL POINTS

Remember Rolle's theorem, which states that if two points have the same value in the range that there must be a point between them where the slope of the graph is zero. This point is located at a peak or valley on the graph. A **peak** is a maximum point, and a **valley** is a minimum point. The relative minimum is the lowest point on a graph for a given section of the graph. It may or may not be the same as the absolute minimum, which is the lowest point on the entire graph. The relative maximum is the highest point on one section of the graph. Again, it may or may not be the same as the absolute maximum. A relative extremum (plural extrema) is a relative minimum or relative maximum point on a graph.

A **critical point** is a point $(x, f(x))$ that is part of the domain of a function, such that either $f'(x) = 0$ or $f'(x)$ does not exist. If either of these conditions is true, then x is either an inflection point or a point at which the slope of the curve changes sign. If the slope changes sign, then a relative minimum or maximum occurs.

In graphing an equation with relative extrema, use a sign diagram to approximate the shape of the graph. Once you have determined the relative extrema, calculate the sign of a point on either side of each critical point. This will give a general shape of the graph, and you will know whether each critical point is a relative minimum, a relative maximum, or a point of inflection.

FIRST DERIVATIVE TEST

Remember that critical points occur where the slope of the curve is 0. Also remember that the **first derivative** of a function gives the slope of the curve at a particular point on the curve. Because of this property of the first derivative, the first derivative test can be used to determine if a critical point is a minimum or maximum. If $f'(x)$ is negative at a point to the left of a critical number and $f'(x)$ is positive at a point to the right of a critical number, then the critical number is a relative minimum. If $f'(x)$ is positive to the left of a critical number and $f'(x)$ is negative to the right of a critical number, then the critical number is a relative maximum. If $f'(x)$ has the same sign on both sides, then the critical number is a point of inflection.

SECOND DERIVATIVE TEST

The **second derivative**, designated by $f''(x)$, is helpful in determining whether the relative extrema of a function are relative maximums or relative minimums. If the second derivative at the critical point is greater than zero, the critical point is a relative minimum. If the second derivative at the critical point is less than zero, the critical point is a relative maximum. If the second derivative at the critical point is equal to zero, you must use the first derivative test to determine whether the point is a relative minimum or a relative maximum.

There are a couple of ways to determine the concavity of the graph of a function. To test a portion of the graph that contains a point with domain p, find the second derivative of the function and evaluate it for p. If $f''(p) > 0$, then the graph is concave upward at that point. If $f''(p) < 0$, then the graph is concave downward at that point.

The **point of inflection** on the graph of a function is the point at which the concavity changes from concave downward to concave upward or from concave upward to concave downward. The easiest way to find the points of inflection is to find the second derivative of the function and then solve the equation $f''(x) = 0$. Remember that if $f''(p) > 0$, the graph is concave upward, and if $f''(p) < 0$, the graph is concave downward. Logically, the concavity changes at the point when $f''(p) = 0$:

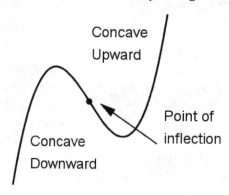

The derivative tests that have been discussed thus far can help you get a rough picture of what the graph of an unfamiliar function looks like. Begin by solving the equation $f(x) = 0$ to find all the zeros of the function, if they exist. Plot these points on the graph. Then, find the first derivative of the function and solve the equation $f'(x) = 0$ to find the critical points. Remember the numbers obtained here are the x portions of the coordinates. Substitute these values for x in the original function and solve for y to get the full coordinates of the points. Plot these points on the graph. Take the second derivative of the function and solve the equation $f''(x) = 0$ to find the points of inflection. Substitute in the original function to get the coordinates and graph these points. Test points on both sides of the critical points to test for concavity and draw the curve.

DERIVATIVE PROBLEMS

A derivative represents the rate of change of a function; thus, derivatives are a useful tool for solving any problem that involves finding the rate at which a function is changing. In its simplest form, such a problem might provide a formula for a quantity as a function of time and ask for its rate of change at a particular time.

If the temperature in a chamber in degrees Celsius is equal to $T(t) = 20 + e^{-\left(\frac{t}{2}\right)}$, where t is the time in seconds, then the derivative of the function represents the rate of change of the temperature over time. The rate of change is equal to $\frac{dT}{dt} = \frac{d}{dt}\left(20 + e^{-\left(\frac{t}{2}\right)}\right) = -\frac{1}{2}e^{-\left(\frac{t}{2}\right)}$, and the initial rate of change is $T'(0) = -\frac{1}{2}e^{-\left(\frac{0}{2}\right)} = -\frac{1}{2}\frac{°C}{s}$.

Suppose we are told that the net profit that a small company makes when it produces and sells x units of a product is equal to $P(x) = 200x - 20{,}000$. The derivative of this function would be the *additional profit for each additional unit sold*, a quantity known as the marginal profit. The marginal profit in this case is $P'(x) = 200$.

SOLVING RELATED RATES PROBLEMS

A **related rate problem** is one in which one variable has a relation with another variable, and the rate of change of one of the variables is known. With that information, the rate of change of the other variable can be determined. The first step in solving related rates problems is defining the known rate of change. Then, determine the relationship between the two variables, then the derivatives (the rates of change), and finally substitute the problem's specific values. Consider the following example:

The side of a cube is increasing at a rate of 2 feet per second. Determine the rate at which the volume of the cube is increasing when the side of the cube is 4 feet long.

For the problem in question, the known rate of change can be expressed as $s'(t) = \frac{ds}{dt} = 2\frac{ft}{s}$, where s is the length of the side and t is the elapsed time in seconds. The relationship between the two variables of the cube is $v = s^3$, where v is the volume of the cube and s is the length of the side. The unknown rate of change to determine is the volume. As both v and s change with time, $v = s^3$ becomes $v(t) = [s(t)]^3$

Now, the chain rule is applied to differentiate both sides of the equation with respect to t.

$$d\frac{v(t)}{dt} = \frac{d[s(t)]^3}{dt}; \quad \frac{dv}{dt} = \frac{(3[s(t)]^2)ds}{dt}$$

Finally, the specific value of $s = 4$ feet is substituted, and the equation is evaluated.

$$\frac{dv}{dt} = \frac{(3[s(t)]^2)ds}{dt}$$
$$= 3(4)^2 \times 2 = 96\frac{ft^3}{s}$$
$$= 96 \text{ cubic}\frac{ft}{s}$$

Therefore, when a side of the cube is 4 feet long, the volume of the cube is increasing at a rate of 96 cubic $\frac{feet}{second}$.

SOLVING OPTIMIZATION PROBLEMS

An **optimization problem** is a problem in which we are asked to find the value of a variable that maximizes or minimizes a particular value. Because the maximum or maximum occurs at a critical point, and because the critical point occurs when the derivative of the function is zero, we can solve an optimization problem by setting the derivative of the function to zero and solving for the desired variable.

For example, suppose a farmer has 720 m of fencing, and wants to use it to fence in a 2 by 3 block of identical rectangular pens. What dimensions of the pens will maximize their area?

We can draw a diagram:

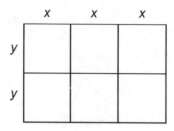

We want to maximize the area of each pen, $A(x, y) = xy$. However, we have the additional constraint that the farmer has only 720 m of fencing. In terms of x and y, we can count the number of segments of each length, 9 for x and 8 for y, so the total amount of fencing required will be $9x + 8y$. Our constraint becomes $9x + 8y = 720$; solving for y yields $y = -\frac{9}{8}x + 90$. We can substitute that into the area equation to get $A(x) = x\left(-\frac{9}{8}x + 90\right) = -\frac{9}{8}x^2 + 90x$. Taking the derivative yields $A'(x) = -\frac{9}{4}x + 90$; setting that equal to zero and solving for x yields $x = 40$. $y = -\frac{9}{8}(40) + 90 = 45$; thus, the maximum dimensions of the pen are 40 by 45 meters.

CHARACTERISTICS OF FUNCTIONS (USING CALCULUS)

Rolle's theorem states that if a differentiable function has two different values in the domain that correspond to a single value in the range, then the function must have a point between them where the slope of the tangent to the graph is zero. This point will be a maximum or a minimum value of the function between those two points. The maximum or minimum point is the point at which $f'(c) = 0$, where c is within the appropriate interval of the function's domain. The following graph shows a function with one maximum in the second quadrant and one minimum in the fourth quadrant.

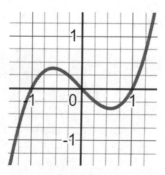

MEAN VALUE THEOREM

According to the **mean value theorem**, between any two points on a curve, there exists a tangent to the curve whose slope is parallel to the chord formed by joining those two points. Remember the formula for slope: $m = \frac{\Delta x}{\Delta y}$. In a function, $f(x)$ represents the value for y. Therefore, if you have two points on a curve, m and n, the corresponding points are $(m, f(m))$ and $(n, f(n))$. Assuming $m < n$, the formula for the slope of the chord joining those two points is $\frac{f(n)-f(m)}{n-m}$. This must also be the slope of a line parallel to the chord, since parallel lines have equal slopes. Therefore, there must be a value p between m and n such that $f'(p) = \frac{f(n)-f(m)}{n-m}$.

For a function to have continuity, its graph must be an unbroken curve. That is, it is a function that can be graphed without having to lift the pencil to move it to a different point. To say a function is continuous at point p, you must show the function satisfies three requirements. First, $f(p)$ must exist. If you evaluate the function at p, it must yield a real number. Second, there must exist a relationship such that $\lim_{x \to p} f(x) = f(p)$. Finally, the following relationship must be true:

$$\lim_{x \to p^+} F(x) = \lim_{x \to p^-} F(x) = F(p)$$

If all three of these requirements are met, a function is considered continuous at p. If any one of them is not true, the function is not continuous at p.

Review Video: Mean Value Theorem
Visit mometrix.com/academy and enter code: 633482

TANGENTS

Tangents are lines that touch a curve in exactly one point and have the same slope as the curve at that point. To find the slope of a curve at a given point and the slope of its tangent line at that point, find the derivative of the function of the curve. If the slope is undefined, the tangent is a vertical line. If the slope is zero, the tangent is a horizontal line.

A line that is normal to a curve at a given point is perpendicular to the tangent at that point. Assuming $f'(x) \neq 0$, the equation for the normal line at point (a, b) is: $y - b = -\frac{1}{f'(a)}(x - a)$. The easiest way to find the slope of the normal is to take the negative reciprocal of the slope of the tangent. If the slope of the tangent is zero, the slope of the normal is undefined. If the slope of the tangent is undefined, the slope of the normal is zero.

ANTIDERIVATIVES (INTEGRALS)

The antiderivative of a function is the function whose first derivative is the original function. Antiderivatives are typically represented by capital letters, while their first derivatives are represented by lower case letters. For example, if $F' = f$, then F is the antiderivative of f. Antiderivatives are also known as indefinite integrals. When taking the derivative of a function, any constant terms in the function are eliminated because their derivative is 0. To account for this possibility, when you take the indefinite integral of a function, you must add an unknown constant C to the end of the function. Because there is no way to know what the value of the original constant was when looking just at the first derivative, the integral is indefinite.

To find the indefinite integral, reverse the process of differentiation. Below are the formulas for constants and powers of x.

$$\int 0 \, dx = C$$

$$\int k \, dx = kx + C$$

$$\int x^n \, dx = \frac{x^{n+1}}{n+1} + C, \text{where } n \neq -1$$

Recall that in the differentiation of powers of x, you multiplied the coefficient of the term by the exponent of the variable and then reduced the exponent by one. In integration, the process is reversed: add one to the value of the exponent, and then divide the coefficient of the term by this number to get the integral. Because you do not know the value of any constant term that might have been in the original function, add C to the end of the function once you have completed this process for each term.

Review Video: <u>Indefinite Integrals</u>
Visit mometrix.com/academy and enter code: 541913

Finding the integral of a function is the opposite of finding the derivative of the function. Where possible, you can use the trigonometric or logarithmic differentiation formulas in reverse, and add C to the end to compensate for the unknown term. In instances where a negative sign appears in the differentiation formula, move the negative sign to the opposite side (multiply both sides by -1) to reverse for the integration formula. You should end up with the following formulas:

$$\int \cos x \, dx = \sin x + C \qquad \int \sec^2 x \, dx = \tan x + C$$

$$\int \sec x \tan x \, dx = \sec x + C \qquad \int \csc^2 x \, dx = -\cot x + C$$

$$\int \sin x \, dx = -\cos x + C \qquad \int \frac{1}{x} \, dx = \ln|x| + C$$

$$\int \csc x \cot x \, dx = -\csc x + C \qquad \int e^x \, dx = e^x + C$$

Integration by substitution is the integration version of the chain rule for differentiation. The formula for integration by substitution is given by the equation

$$f(g(x))g'(x)dx = \int f(u)du; \quad u = g(x) \text{ and } du = g'(x)dx$$

When a function is in a format that is difficult or impossible to integrate using traditional integration methods and formulas due to multiple functions being combined, use the formula shown above to convert the function to a simpler format that can be integrated directly.

Integration by parts is the integration version of the product rule for differentiation. Whenever you are asked to find the integral of the product of two different functions or parts, integration by parts can make the process simpler. Recall for differentiation $(fg)'(x) = f(x)g'(x) + g(x)f'(x)$. This can also be written $\frac{d}{dx}(u \times v) = u\frac{dv}{dx} + v\frac{du}{dx}$, where $u = f(x)$ and $v = g(x)$. Rearranging to integral form gives the formula:

$$\int u\, dv = uv - \int v\, du$$
$$\int f(x)g'(x)\, dx = f(x)g(x) - \int f'(x)g(x)\, dx$$

When using integration by parts, the key is selecting the best functions to substitute for u and v so that you make the integral easier to solve and not harder.

While the indefinite integral has an undefined constant added at the end, the definite integral can be calculated as an exact real number. To find the definite integral of a function over a closed interval, use the formula $\int_n^m f(x)\, dx = F(m) - F(n)$ where F is the integral of f. Because you have been given the boundaries of n and m, no undefined constant C is needed.

> **Review Video: Integration by Parts**
> Visit mometrix.com/academy and enter code: 459972
>
> **Review Video: Integration by Substitution**
> Visit mometrix.com/academy and enter code: 740649

FIRST FUNDAMENTAL THEOREM OF CALCULUS

The **first fundamental theorem of calculus** shows that the process of indefinite integration can be reversed by finding the first derivative of the resulting function. It also gives the relationship between differentiation and integration over a closed interval of the function. For example, assuming a function is continuous over the interval $[m, n]$, you can find the definite integral by using the formula

$$\int_m^n f(x)\, dx = F(n) - F(m)$$

To find the **average value** of the function over the given interval, use the formula:

$$\frac{1}{n-m}\int_m^n f(x)\, dx$$

> **Review Video: First Fundamental Theorem of Calculus**
> Visit mometrix.com/academy and enter code: 248431

SECOND FUNDAMENTAL THEOREM OF CALCULUS

The **second fundamental theorem of calculus** is related to the first. This theorem states that, assuming the function is continuous over the interval you are considering, taking the derivative of the integral of a function will yield the original function. The general format for this theorem for any point having a domain value equal to c in the given interval is:

$$\frac{d}{dx}\int_c^x f(x)\, dx = f(x)$$

For each of the following **properties of integrals** of function f, the variables $m, n,$ and p represent values in the domain of the given interval of $f(x)$. The function is assumed to be integrable across all relevant intervals.

Swapping the limits of integration:
$$\int_m^n f(x)\, dx = -\int_n^m f(x)\, dx$$

Function multiplied by a constant:
$$\int_m^n kf(x)dx = k\int_m^n f(x)\, dx$$

Separating the integral into parts:
$$\int_m^n f(x)\, dx = \int_m^p f(x)\, dx + \int_p^n f(x)\, dx$$

If the limits of integration are equivalent:
$$\int_n^n f(x)\, dx = 0$$

If $f(x)$ is an even function and the limits of integration are symmetric:
$$\int_{-m}^m f(x)\, dx = 2\int_0^m f(x)\, dx$$

If $f(x)$ is an odd function and the limits of integration are symmetric:
$$\int_{-m}^m f(x)\, dx = 0$$

Review Video: Second Fundamental Theorem of Calculus
Visit mometrix.com/academy and enter code: 524689

MATCHING FUNCTIONS TO DERIVATIVES OR ACCUMULATIONS
DERIVATIVES

We can use what we know about the meaning of a derivative to match the graph of a function with a graph of its derivative. For one thing, we know that where the function has a critical point, the derivative is zero. Therefore, at every x value at which the graph of a function has a maximum or minimum, the derivative must cross the x-axis—and conversely, everywhere the graph of the derivative crosses the x axis, the function must have a critical point: either a maximum, a minimum, or an inflection point. If this is still not enough to identify the correct match, we can also use the fact that the sign of the derivative corresponds to whether the function is increasing or decreasing: everywhere the graph of the derivative is above the x-axis, the function must be increasing (its slope is positive), and everywhere the graph of the derivative is below the x-axis, the function must be decreasing (its slope is negative).

For example, below are graphs of the function and its derivative. The maxima and minima of the function (left) are circled, and the zeroes of the derivative (right) are circled.

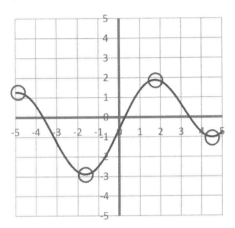 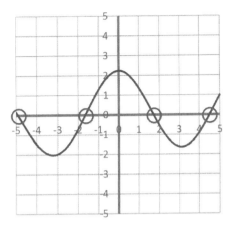

ACCUMULATIONS

The **accumulation** of a function is another name for its antiderivative, or integral. We can use the relationship between a function and its antiderivative to match the corresponding graphs. For example, we know that where the graph of the function is above the x-axis, the function is positive, thus the accumulation must be increasing (its slope is positive); where the graph of the function is below the x-axis, the accumulation must be decreasing (its slope is negative). It follows that where the function changes from positive to negative—where the graph crosses the x-axis with a negative slope—, its accumulation changes from increasing to decreasing—so the accumulation has a local maximum. Where the function changes from negative to positive—where its graph crosses the x-axis with a positive slope—, the accumulation has a local minimum.

For example, below are graphs of a function and its accumulation. The points on the function (left) where the graph crosses the x-axis are circled; the local minima and maxima of the accumulation (right) are circled.

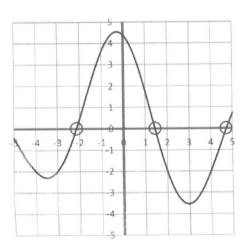 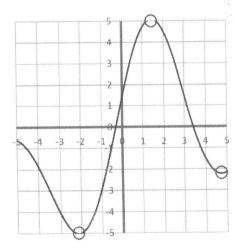

RIEMANN SUMS

A **Riemann sum** is a sum used to approximate the definite integral of a function over a particular interval by dividing the area under the function into vertical rectangular strips and adding the areas of the strips. The height of each strip is equal to the value of the function at some point within the interval covered by the strip. Formally, if we divide the interval over which we are finding the area into n intervals bounded by the $n + 1$ points $\{x_i\}$ (where x_0 and x_n are the left and right bounds of the interval), then the Riemann sum is $\sum_{i=1}^{n} f(x_i^*)\Delta x_i$, where $\Delta x_i = x_i - x_{i-1}$ and x_i^* is some point in the interval $[x_{i-1}, x_i]$. In principle, any point in the interval can be chosen, but common choices include the left endpoint of the interval (yielding the **left Riemann sum**), the right endpoint (yielding the **right Riemann sum**), and the midpoint of the interval (the basis of the **midpoint rule**). Usually, it is convenient to set all the intervals to the same width, although the definition of the Riemann sum does not require this.

The following graphic shows the rectangular strips used for one possible Riemann sum of a particular function:

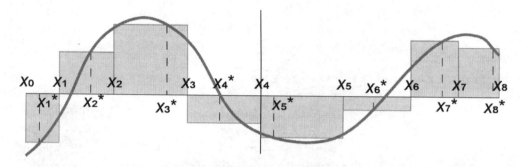

| Review Video: **Midpoint Rule** |
| Visit mometrix.com/academy and enter code: 790070 |

LEFT AND RIGHT RIEMANN SUMS

A **Riemann sum** is an approximation to the definite integral of a function over a particular interval performed by dividing it into smaller intervals and summing the products of the width of each interval and the value of the function evaluated at some point within the interval. The **left Riemann sum** is a Riemann sum in which the function is evaluated at the left endpoint of each interval. In the **right Riemann sum**, the function is evaluated at the right endpoint of each interval.

When the function is increasing, the left Riemann sum will always underestimate the function. This is because we are evaluating the function at the minimum point within each interval; the integral of the function in the interval will be larger than the estimate. Conversely, the right Riemann sum is evaluating the function at the maximum point within each interval, thus it will always overestimate the function. Consider the following diagrams, in which the area under the same increasing function is shown approximated by a left Riemann sum and a right Riemann sum:

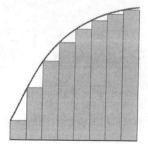 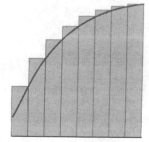

For a decreasing function these considerations are reversed: a left Riemann sum will overestimate the integral, and a right Riemann sum will underestimate it.

MIDPOINT RULE

The **midpoint rule** is a way of approximating the definite integral of a function over an interval by dividing the interval into smaller sub-intervals, multiplying the width of each sub-interval by the value of the function at the midpoint of the sub-interval, and then summing these products. This is a special case of the Riemann sum, specifying the midpoint of the interval as the point at which the function is to be evaluated. The approximation found using the midpoint rule is usually more accurate than that found using the left or right Riemann sum, though as the number of intervals becomes very large the difference becomes negligible.

For example, suppose we are asked to estimate by the midpoint rule the integral of $f(x) = \frac{1}{x}$ in the interval $[2, 4]$. We can divide this interval into four intervals of width $\frac{1}{2}$: $[2, 2.5]$, $[2.5, 3]$, $[3, 3.5]$, and $[3.5, 4]$. (The more intervals, the more accurate the estimate, but we'll use a small number of intervals in this example to keep it simple.) The midpoint rule then gives an estimate of

$$\frac{1}{2}\left(f(2.25)\right) + \frac{1}{2}\left(f(2.75)\right) + \frac{1}{2}\left(f(3.25)\right) + \frac{1}{2}\left(f(3.75)\right) = \frac{1}{2}\left(\frac{4}{9}\right) + \frac{1}{2}\left(\frac{4}{11}\right) + \frac{1}{2}\left(\frac{4}{13}\right) + \frac{1}{2}\left(\frac{4}{15}\right) \approx 0.691, \text{ not}$$

far from the actual value of $\int_2^4 \frac{1}{x}dx = [\ln x]_2^4 \approx 0.693$.

TRAPEZOID RULE

The **trapezoid rule** is a method of approximating the definite integral of a function by dividing the area under the function into a series of trapezoidal strips, the upper corners of the trapezoid touching the function, and adding the areas of the strips. The following diagram shows the use of the trapezoid rule to estimate the integral of the function $y = 2^x$ in the interval $[0, 3]$:

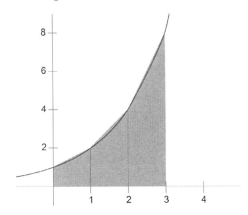

Mathematically, if we define the endpoints of the n subdivisions to be $\{x_i\}$, where x_0 and x_n are the endpoints of the entire interval over which we are estimating the integral, then the result of the application of the trapezoid rule is equal to $\sum_{i=1}^{n} \left(\frac{x_{i-1}+x_i}{2}\right)(x_i - x_{i-1})$. For the example shown above, that yields $\left(\frac{2^1+2^0}{2}\right)(1 - 0) + \left(\frac{2^2+2^1}{2}\right)(2 - 1) + \left(\frac{2^3+2^2}{2}\right)(3 - 2) = \frac{21}{2}$, or 10.5—not far from the actual value of $\int_0^3 2^x dx = \int_0^3 e^{x\ln 2}\, dx = \left[\frac{2^x}{\ln 2}\right]_0^3 \approx 10.1$. (Of course, we could have achieved more accuracy by using smaller subdivisions.)

The trapezoid rule is related to the Riemann sum, but usually gives more accurate results than the left or right Riemann sum for the same number of intervals. In fact, it isn't hard to prove that the answer given by the trapezoid rule is equal to the average of the left and right Riemann sums using the same partition.

LIMIT OF RIEMANN SUMS

As the number of sub-intervals becomes larger, and the width of each sub-interval becomes smaller, the approximation becomes increasingly accurate, and at the limit as the number of sub-intervals approaches infinity and their width approaches zero, the value becomes exact. In fact, the definite integral is often defined as a limit of Riemann sums.

It's possible to find the definite integral by this method. Suppose we want to find the integral of $f(x) = x^2$ over the interval $[0, 2]$. We'll divide this interval into n sub-intervals of equal width and evaluate the function at the right endpoint of each sub-interval. (This choice is arbitrary; at the limit the answer would be the same if we chose the left endpoint, or any other point within the interval.)

Our Riemann sum becomes $\sum_{i=1}^{n} \frac{2}{n} \left(\frac{2}{n}i\right)^2 = \frac{8}{n^3} \sum_{i=1}^{n} i^2$, where $\sum_{i=1}^{n} i^2 = \frac{1}{6}n(n+1)(2n+1)$, thus this becomes $\frac{8}{n^3} \cdot \frac{1}{6}n(n+1)(2n+1) = \frac{4}{3}\left(1 + \frac{1}{n}\right)\left(2 + \frac{1}{n}\right)$. At the limit as $n \to \infty$, this becomes $\frac{4}{3}(1)(2) = \frac{8}{3}$. This is the same result as we get by integrating directly: $\int_0^2 x^2 dx = \left[\frac{1}{3}x^3\right]_0^2 = \frac{1}{3}(2)^3 - \frac{1}{3}(0)^3 = \frac{8}{3}$.

USES FOR INTEGRATION

CALCULATING DISTANCES

When given the velocity of an object over time, it's possible to find a distance by integration. The velocity is the rate of change of the position; therefore, the displacement is the accumulation of the velocity: that is, the integral of the velocity is the displacement. However, if asked to find the total distance traveled (as opposed to the displacement), it's important to take the sign into account: we must integrate not just the velocity, but the absolute value of the velocity, which essentially means integrating separately over each interval in which the velocity has a different sign.

For example, suppose we're asked to find the total distance traveled from $t = 0$ to $t = 8$ by an object moving with a velocity in meters per second given by the equation $v(t) = 2\sqrt{t} - t$. This function is zero when $2\sqrt{t} - t = 0 \Rightarrow \sqrt{t}(2 - \sqrt{t}) = 0 \Rightarrow t = 0$ or 4. $v(t)$ is positive when $0 < t < 4$ and negative when $t > 4$. Thus, the distance travelled is

$$\int_0^8 |v(t)|dt = \int_0^8 |2\sqrt{t} - t|dt$$

$$= \int_0^4 (2\sqrt{t} - t)dt - \int_4^8 (2\sqrt{t} - t)dt$$

$$= \left[\frac{4}{3}t^{\frac{3}{2}} - \frac{1}{2}t^2\right]_0^4 - \left[\frac{4}{3}t^{\frac{3}{2}} - \frac{1}{2}t^2\right]_4^8$$

$$= \left(\left[\frac{4}{3}(4)^{\frac{3}{2}} - \frac{1}{2}4^2\right] - \left[\frac{4}{3}(0)^{\frac{3}{2}} - \frac{1}{2}(0)^2\right]\right) - \left(\left[\frac{4}{3}(8)^{\frac{3}{2}} - \frac{1}{2}(8)^2\right] - \left[\frac{4}{3}(4)^{\frac{3}{2}} - \frac{1}{2}(4)^2\right]\right)$$

$$= \left(\left[\frac{32}{3} - 8\right] - 0\right) - \left(\left[\frac{64}{3}\sqrt{2} - 32\right] - \left[\frac{32}{3} - 8\right]\right)$$

$$= \frac{8}{3} - \frac{64}{3}\sqrt{2} + \frac{96}{3} + \frac{8}{3}$$

$$= \frac{8}{3}(1 - 8\sqrt{2} + 12 + 1)$$

$$= \frac{8}{3}(14 - 8\sqrt{2}) \approx 7.16 \text{ meters}$$

CALCULATING AREAS

One way to calculate the area of an irregular shape is to find a formula for the width of the shape along the x direction as a function of the y coordinate, and then integrate over y, or vice versa. What this amounts to is dividing the area into thin strips and adding the areas of the strips—and then taking the limit as the width of the strips approaches zero.

For example, suppose we want to find the area enclosed by the functions $y_1 = x^2$ and $y_2 = (2 - x^2)$. The height of this enclosure is equal to $y_2 - y_1 = 2 - 2x^2$; we can find the area by integrating this height over x. The two shapes intersect at the points $(1, 1)$ and $(-1, 1)$, thus our limits of integration are –1 and 1. Thus the area can be found as:

$$\int_{-1}^1 (2 - 2x^2)dx = \left[2x - \frac{2}{3}x^3\right]_{-1}^1 = \left(2(1) - \frac{2}{3}(1)\right) - \left(2(-1) - \frac{2}{3}(-1)\right) = \frac{8}{3}$$

CALCULATING VOLUMES

One way to calculate the volume of a three-dimensional shape is to find a formula for its cross-sectional area perpendicular to some axis and then integrate over that axis. Effectively, this divides the shape into thin, flat slices and adds the volumes of the slices—and then takes the limit as the thickness of the slices approaches zero.

For example, suppose we want to find the area of the ellipsoid $4x^2 + 4y^2 + z^2 = 36$. If we take a cross-section parallel to the z-axis, this has the formula $4x^2 + 4y^2 = 36 - z^2$, or $x^2 + y^2 = 9 - \frac{z^2}{4}$; this is the formula of a circle with a radius of $\sqrt{9 - \frac{z^2}{4}}$, and thus has an area of $\pi\left(9 - \frac{z^2}{4}\right)$. To find the volume, we integrate this formula over z. The maximum and minimum values of z occur when $x = y = 0$, and then $z^2 = 36$, thus $z = \pm 6$; these are our limits of integration. Thus, the volume is:

$$\int_{-6}^{6} \pi \left(9 - \frac{z^2}{4}\right) dz = \pi \left[9z - \frac{z^3}{12}\right]_{-6}^{6}$$
$$= \pi\left[\left(9(6) - \frac{6^3}{12}\right) - \left(9(-6) - \frac{(-6)^3}{12}\right)\right]$$
$$= \pi[(54 - 18) - (-54 + 18)]$$
$$= 72\pi \approx 226.2$$

PRACTICE

P1. Evaluate $\lim_{x \to 4} f(x)$ for the following functions:

(a) $f(x) = 7$

(b) $f(x) = \frac{x-4}{x^2-16}$

(c) $f(x) = \begin{cases} x + 1, \text{ when } x < 4 \\ x - 1, \text{ when } x \geq 4 \end{cases}$

P2. Given that $\lim_{x \to 3} f(x) = 2$, $\lim_{x \to 3} g(x) = 6$, and $k = 5$, solve the following:

(a) $\lim_{x \to 3} kg(x)$

(b) $\lim_{x \to 3}(f(x) + g(x))$

(c) $\lim_{x \to 3} f(x) \times g(x)$

(d) $\lim_{x \to 3} g(x) \div f(x)$

(e) $\lim_{x \to 3}[f(x)]^n = C^n$, where $n = 3$

P3. Find $f'(x)$ for the following functions:

(a) $f(x) = 3x$

(b) $f(x) = x^2$

P4. Use the power rule of differentiation to differentiate the following:

(a) $f(x) = 4x^2$

(b) $f(x) = x^4$

(c) $f(x) = 3x^2 - 5x + 6$

68

P5. Calculate the area under the curve of the function $f(x) = x^2 + 3$ on the interval $[2,5]$ using:

(a) right-hand approximation with 6 subdivisions.

(b) left-hand approximation with 3 subdivisions.

P6. Find the position, velocity, and acceleration for the following at $t = 3$ s:

(a) A train begins moving and its displacement (in meters) is: $s(t) = t^2 + 4t + 5$

(b) A car begins moving and its displacement (in feet) is: $s(t) = t^3$

P7. Find $\frac{dy}{dx}$ given the equation $xy^2 = 3y + 2x$.

P8. Use the first fundamental theorem of calculus to evaluate:

(a) $\int_0^1 (x^3 + 2x)dx$

(b) $\int_{-1}^0 (3x^2 + 2)dx$

P9. Find the total distance traveled from $t = 0$ to $t = 10$ by an object moving with a velocity in meters per second given by the equation $v(t) = 6t - t^2$.

PRACTICE SOLUTIONS

P1. (a) 7 is a constant function, so therefore, $\lim_{x \to 4} 7 = 7$

(b) $\lim_{x \to 4} \frac{x-4}{x^2-16}$ can be simplified by factoring:

$$\lim_{x \to 4} \frac{x-4}{x^2-16} = \lim_{x \to 4} \frac{x-4}{(x+4)(x-4)} = \lim_{x \to 4} \frac{1}{x+4} = \frac{1}{8}$$

(c) $\lim_{x \to 4} f(x)$, when $f(x) = x + 1$ for $x < 4$ and $f(x) = x - 1$ for $x \geq 4$

$$\lim_{x \to 4^+} f(x) = x - 1 = 4 - 1 = 3$$
$$\lim_{x \to 4^-} f(x) = x + 1 = 4 + 1 = 5$$

Therefore, $\lim_{x \to 4} f(x)$, does not exist.

P2. (a) $\lim_{x \to a} kf(x) = kC$, where k is a constant, so $\lim_{x \to 3} kg(x) = 5 \times 6 = 30$

(b) $\lim_{x \to a}(f(x) \pm g(x)) = C \pm D$, so $\lim_{x \to 3}(f(x) + g(x)) = 2 + 6 = 8$

(c) $\lim_{x \to a} f(x) \times g(x) = C \times D$, so $\lim_{x \to 3} f(x) \times g(x) = 2 \times 6 = 12$

(d) $\lim_{x \to a} f(x) \div g(x) = C \div D$, if $D \neq 0$, so $\lim_{x \to 3} \frac{g(x)}{f(x)} = \frac{6}{2} = 3$

(e) $\lim_{x \to a}[f(x)]^n = C^n$, so $\lim_{x \to 3}[f(x)]^n = C^n = 2^3 = 8$

$$f'(x) = \lim_{h \to 0} \frac{f(x+h) - f(x)}{h}:$$

$$\lim_{t \to 0} \frac{3x + 3h - 3x}{h}$$

$$= \lim_{h \to 0} \frac{3h}{h}$$

$$= \lim_{h \to 0} 3$$

$$= 3$$

(b)
$$f'(x) = \lim_{h \to 0} \frac{x^2 + 2xh + h^2 - x^2}{h}$$

$$= \lim_{h \to 0} \frac{2xh + h^2}{h}$$

$$= \lim_{h \to 0} 2x + h$$

$$= 2x$$

P4. The power rule is useful for finding the derivative of polynomial functions. It states that the derivative of $x^n = nx^{n-1}$.

(a) $f(x) = 4x^2 \to f'(x) = 2 \times 4x^2 - 1 = 8x$

(b) $f(x) = x^4 \to f'(x) = 4 \times x^{4-1} = 4x^3$

(c) $f(x) = 3x^2 - 5x + 6 \to f'(x) = 2 \times 3x^{2-1} - 1 \times 5x^{1-1} = 6x - 5$

P5. (a) First, divide the interval [2,5] by the number of subdivisions, $\Delta x = \frac{b-a}{n} = \frac{5-2}{6} = 0.5$, thus each rectangle has a width of 0.5.

The height of the right-hand side of each rectangle is given by the value of the function at the points $x = 2.5, 3, 3.5, 4, 4.5, 5$. Summing these heights and multiplying by the width of each rectangle gives the approximate total area under the curve.

$$= 0.5\big(f(2.5) + f(3) + f(3.5) + f(4) + f(4.5) + f(5)\big)$$
$$= 0.5(9.25 + 12 + 15.25 + 19 + 23.25 + 28) = 53.375$$

The total area under the curve of the function $f(x) = x^2 + 3$ on the interval [2,5], calculated using right-hand approximation, is found to be approximately 53.375.

(b) First, divide the interval [2,5] by the number of subdivisions, $\Delta x = \frac{b-a}{n} = \frac{5-2}{3} = 1$, thus each rectangle has a width of 1.

The height of the left-hand side of each rectangle is given by the value of the function at $x = 2, 3, 4$. Summing these heights and multiplying by the width of each rectangle gives the approximate area under the curve.

$$1\big(f(2) + f(3) + f(4)\big) = (7 + 12 + 19) = 38$$

The total area under the curve of the function $f(x) = x^2 + 3$ on the interval [2,5], calculated using left-hand approximation, is found to be approximately 38.

P6. Find each derivative and evaluate at $t = 3$:

(a) $s(t) = t^2 + 4t + 5$ $v(t) = s'(t) = 2t + 4$ $a(t) = v'(t) = 2$

$$s(3) = 3^2 + 4(3) + 5$$
$$= 26 \text{ m}$$

$$v(3) = 2(3) + 4$$
$$= 10 \frac{m}{s}$$

$$a(3) = 2 \frac{m}{s^2}$$

(b) $s(t) = t^3$ $v(t) = s'(t) = 3t^2$ $a(t) = v'(t) = 6t$

$$s(3) = 3^3$$
$$= 27 \text{ ft}$$

$$v(3) = 3(3)^2$$
$$= 27 \frac{ft}{s}$$

$$a(3) = 6(3)$$
$$= 18 \frac{ft}{s^2}$$

P7. Take the derivative of each term with respect to x: $\frac{d}{dx}(xy^2) = \frac{d}{dx}(3y + 2x)$. In order to take the derivative of the left side, we will need to use the product rule $\left(\frac{d}{dx}(u \times v) = v\frac{du}{dx} + u\frac{dv}{dx}\right)$ where $u = x$ and $v = y^2$:

$$\frac{d}{dx}(x)y^2 + \frac{d}{dx}(y^2)x = \frac{d}{dx}(3y + 2x)$$
$$y^2 + \frac{d}{dx}(y^2)x = \frac{d}{dx}(3y) + \frac{d}{dx}(2x)$$

Now we will use the chain rule $\left(\frac{d}{dx}f(u) = \frac{df}{du} \times \frac{du}{dx}\right)$ where $f(u) = y^2$ and $u = y$:

$$y^2 + \left(\frac{d(y^2)}{dy} \times \frac{dy}{dx}\right)x = \frac{d}{dx}(3y) + \frac{d}{dx}(2x)$$
$$y^2 + \left(2y\frac{dy}{dx}\right)x = \frac{d}{dx}(3y) + \frac{d}{dx}(2x)$$
$$y^2 + 2xy\frac{dy}{dx} = 3\frac{dy}{dx} + 2$$
$$2xy\frac{dy}{dx} - 3\frac{dy}{dx} = 2 - y^2$$
$$\frac{dy}{dx} = \frac{2 - y^2}{2xy - 3}$$

P8. (a) By the first fundamental theorem of calculus: $\int_a^b f(x)dx = F(b) - F(a)$

$$\int_0^1 (x^3 + 2x)dx = \left[\frac{x^4}{4} + x^2\right]_{x=0}^1$$
$$= \frac{(1)^4}{4} + (1)^2 - \left(\frac{(0)^4}{4} + (0)^2\right)$$
$$= \frac{5}{4} - 0 = \frac{5}{4}$$

(b) By the first fundamental theorem of calculus: $\int_a^b f(x)dx = F(b) - F(a)$

$$\int_{-1}^{0} (3x^2 + 2)dx = [x^3 + 2x]_{x=-1}^{0}$$
$$= (0)^3 + 2(0) - ((-1)^3 + 2(-1))$$
$$= 0 - (-3) = 3$$

P9. This velocity function is zero when $6t - t^2 = 0 \Rightarrow t(6 - t) = 0 \Rightarrow t = 0$ or 6. $v(t)$ is positive when $0 < t < 6$ and negative when $t > 6$. Thus, the distance travelled is

$$\int_0^{10} |v(t)|dt = \int_0^{10} |6t - t^2|dt$$

$$= \int_0^6 (6t - t^2)dt - \int_6^{10} (6t - t^2)dt$$

$$= \left[3t^2 - \frac{t^3}{3}\right]_0^6 - \left[3t^2 - \frac{t^3}{3}\right]_6^{10}$$

$$= \left(\left[3(6)^2 - \frac{(6)^3}{3}\right] - \left[3(0)^2 - \frac{(0)^3}{3}\right]\right) - \left(\left[3(10)^2 - \frac{(10)^3}{3}\right] - \left[3(6)^2 - \frac{(6)^3}{3}\right]\right)$$

$$= ([108 - 72] - [0]) - \left(\left[300 - \frac{1000}{3}\right] - [108 - 72]\right)$$

$$= 36 - \left[\frac{900}{3} - \frac{1000}{3}\right] + 36$$

$$= 72 - \left[-\frac{100}{3}\right] \approx 105.3 \text{ meters}$$

OAE Practice Test

1. Determine the number of diagonals of a dodecagon.

    a. 12
    b. 24
    c. 54
    d. 108

2. A circular bracelet contains 5 charms, A, B, C, D, and E, attached at specific points around the bracelet, with the clasp located between charms A and B. The bracelet is unclasped and stretched out into a straight line. On the resulting linear bracelet, charm C is between charms A and B, charm D is between charms A and C, and charm E is between charms C and D. Which of these statements is (are) necessarily true?

    I. The distance between charms B and E is greater than the distance between charms A and D.
    II. Charm E is between charms B and D.
    III. The distance between charms D and E is less than the distance of bracelet between charms A and C.

    a. I, II, and III
    b. II and III
    c. II only
    d. None of these must be true.

3. In a town of 35,638 people, about a quarter of the population is under the age of 35. Of those, just over a third attend local K-12 schools. If the number of students in each grade is about the same, how many fourth graders likely reside in the town?

    a. Fewer than 100
    b. Between 200 and 300
    c. Between 300 and 400
    d. More than 400

4. Identical rugs are offered for sale at two local shops and one online retailer, designated Stores A, B, and C, respectively. The rug's regular sales price is $296 at Store A, $220 at Store B, and $198.00 at Store C. Stores A and B collect 8% in sales tax on any after-discount price, while Store C collects no tax but charges a $35 shipping fee. A buyer has a 30% off coupon for Store A and a $10 off coupon for Store B. Which of these lists the stores in order of lowest to highest final sales price after all discounts, taxes, and fees are applied?

    a. Store A, Store B, Store C
    b. Store B, Store C, Store A
    c. Store C, Store A, Store C
    d. Store C, Store B, Store A

5. Two companies offer monthly cell phone plans, both of which include free text messaging. Company A charges a $25 monthly fee plus five cents per minute of phone conversation, while Company B charges a $50 monthly fee and offers unlimited calling. At what total duration of monthly calls do both companies charge the same amount?

    a. 500 hours
    b. 8 hours and 33 minutes
    c. 8 hours and 20 minutes
    d. 5 hours

6. A dress is marked down by 20% and placed on a clearance rack, on which is posted a sign reading, "Take an extra 25% off already reduced merchandise." What fraction of the original price is the final sale price of the dress?

    a. $\frac{9}{20}$
    b. $\frac{11}{20}$
    c. $\frac{2}{5}$
    d. $\frac{3}{5}$

7. On a floor plan drawn at a scale of 1:100, the area of a rectangular room is 30 cm^2. What is the actual area of the room?

    a. 30,000 cm^2
    b. 300 m^2
    c. 3,000 m^2
    d. 30 m^2

8. The ratio of employee wages and benefits to all other operational costs of a business is 2:3. If a business's total operating expenses are $130,000 per month, how much money does the company spend on employee wages and benefits?

    a. $43,333.33
    b. $86,666.67
    c. $52,000.00
    d. $78,000.00

9. The path of a ball thrown into the air is modeled by the first quadrant graph of the equation $h = -18t^2 + 72t + 4$, where h is the height of the ball in feet and t is time in seconds after the ball is thrown. What is the average rate of change in the ball's height with respect to time over the interval $[0, 3]$?

    a. 0 feet/second
    b. 6 feet/second
    c. 18 feet/second
    d. 24 feet/second

10. Zeke drove from his house to a furniture store in Atlanta and then back home along the same route. It took Zeke three hours to drive to the store. By driving an average of 20 mph faster on his return trip, Zeke was able to save an hour of driving time. What was Zeke's average driving speed on his round trip?
   a. 24 mph
   b. 48 mph
   c. 50 mph
   d. 60 mph

11. Aaron goes on a run every morning down the straight country road that he lives on. The graph below shows Aaron's distance from home at times throughout his morning run. Which of the following statements is (are) true?

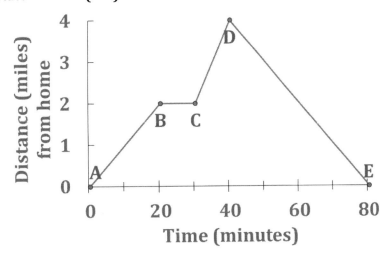

   I. Aaron's average running speed was 6 mph.
   II. Aaron's running speed from A to B was the same as from D to E.
   III. Aaron ran a total distance of four miles.

   a. I only
   b. II only
   c. I and II
   d. I, II, and III

12. Use the operation table to determine $(a * b) * (c * d)$.

*	a	b	c	d
a	d	a	b	c
b	a	b	c	d
c	b	c	d	a
d	c	d	a	b

   a. *a*
   b. *b*
   c. *c*
   d. *d*

13. Complete the analogy: x^3 is to $\sqrt[3]{y}$ as ...

    a. $x + a$ is to $x - y$.
    b. e^x is to $\ln y, y > 0$.
    c. $\frac{1}{x}$ is to $y, x, y \neq 0$.
    d. $\sin x$ is to $\cos y$.

14. Which of these statements is (are) true for deductive reasoning?

    I. A general conclusion is drawn from specific instances.
    II. If the premises are true and proper reasoning is applied, the conclusion must be true.

    a. Statement I is true
    b. Statement II is true
    c. Both statements are true
    d. Neither statement is true

15. Given that premises "all a are b," "all b are d," and "no b are c" are true and that premise "all b are e" is false, determine the validity and soundness of the following arguments:

    Argument I: All a are b. No b are c. Therefore, no a are c.
    Argument II: All a are b. All b are d. Therefore, all d are a.
    Argument III: All a are b. All b are e. Therefore, all a are e.

a.

	Invalid	Valid	Sound
Argument I		X	X
Argument II	X		
Argument III		X	

b.

	Invalid	Valid	Sound
Argument I	X		
Argument II		X	X
Argument III	X		

c.

	Invalid	Valid	Sound
Argument I		X	X
Argument II		X	X
Argument III	X		

d.

	Invalid	Valid	Sound
Argument I		X	X
Argument II	X		
Argument III	X		

16. If $p \rightarrow q$ is true, which of these is also necessarily true?

    a. $q \rightarrow p$
    b. $\neg p \rightarrow \neg q$
    c. $\neg q \rightarrow \neg p$
    d. None of these

17. Given statements p and q, which of the following is the truth table for the statement:

$$q \leftrightarrow \neg(p \wedge q)$$

a.

p	q	$q \leftrightarrow \neg(p \wedge q)$
T	T	F
T	F	T
F	T	T
F	F	T

c.

p	q	$q \leftrightarrow \neg(p \wedge q)$
T	T	F
T	F	F
F	T	F
F	F	T

b.

p	q	$q \leftrightarrow \neg(p \wedge q)$
T	T	T
T	F	T
F	T	T
F	F	F

d.

p	q	$q \leftrightarrow \neg(p \wedge q)$
T	T	F
T	F	F
F	T	T
F	F	F

18. Which of the following is the truth table for logic circuit shown below?

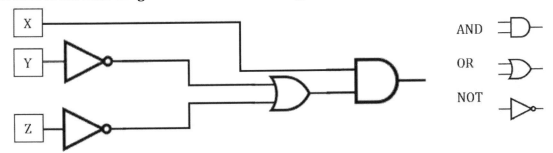

a.

X	Y	Z	Output
0	0	0	1
0	0	1	0
0	1	0	0
0	1	1	0
1	0	0	0
1	0	1	0
1	1	0	0
1	1	1	1

c.

X	Y	Z	Output
0	0	0	0
0	0	1	0
0	1	0	0
0	1	1	1
1	0	0	1
1	0	1	1
1	1	0	1
1	1	1	0

b.

X	Y	Z	Output
0	0	0	0
0	0	1	1
0	1	0	1
0	1	1	1
1	0	0	1
1	0	1	1
1	1	0	1
1	1	1	1

d.

X	Y	Z	Output
0	0	0	0
0	0	1	0
0	1	0	0
0	1	1	0
1	0	0	1
1	0	1	1
1	1	0	1
1	1	1	0

19. Which of these is a major contribution of the Babylonian civilization to the historical development of mathematics?

    a. The division of an hour into 60 minutes, and a minute into 60 seconds, and a circle into 360 degrees

    b. The development of algebra as a discipline separate from geometry

    c. The use of deductive reasoning in geometric proofs

    d. The introduction of Boolean logic

20. Which mathematician is responsible for what is often called the most remarkable and beautiful mathematical formula, $e^{i\pi} + 1 = 0$?

    a. Pythagoras

    b. Euclid

    c. Euler

    d. Fermat

21. Which of these demonstrates the relationship between the sets of prime numbers, real numbers, natural numbers, complex numbers, rational numbers, and integers?

$\mathbb{P}$–Prime; $\mathbb{R}$–Real; $\mathbb{N}$–Natural; $\mathbb{C}$–Complex; $\mathbb{Q}$–Rational; $\mathbb{Z}$–Integer

    a. $\mathbb{P} \subseteq \mathbb{Q} \subseteq \mathbb{R} \subseteq \mathbb{Z} \subseteq \mathbb{C} \subseteq \mathbb{N}$

    b. $\mathbb{P} \subseteq \mathbb{N} \subseteq \mathbb{Z} \subseteq \mathbb{Q} \subseteq \mathbb{R} \subseteq \mathbb{C}$

    c. $\mathbb{C} \subseteq \mathbb{R} \subseteq \mathbb{Q} \subseteq \mathbb{Z} \subseteq \mathbb{N} \subseteq \mathbb{P}$

    d. None of these

22. To which of the following sets of numbers does -4 NOT belong?

    a. The set of whole numbers

    b. The set of rational numbers

    c. The set of integers

    d. The set of real numbers

23. Which of these forms a group?

    a. The set of prime numbers under multiplication

    b. The set of negative integers under subtraction

    c. The set of counting numbers under addition

    d. The set of complex numbers other than zero under multiplication

24. Simplify $\frac{2+3i}{4-2i}$.

    a. $\frac{1}{10} + \frac{4}{5}i$

    b. $\frac{1}{10}$

    c. $\frac{7}{6} + \frac{2}{3}i$

    d. $\frac{1}{10} + \frac{3}{10}i$

25. Simplify $\left|(2 - 3i)^2 - (1 - 4i)\right|$.

    a. $\sqrt{61}$

    b. $-6 - 8i$

    c. $6 + 8i$

    d. 10

26. **Which of these sets forms a group under multiplication?**

    a. $\{-i, 0, i\}$
    b. $\{-1, 1, i, -i\}$
    c. $\{i, 1\}$
    d. $\{i, -i, 1\}$

27. **The set $\{a, b, c, d\}$ forms a group under operation #. Which of these statements is (are) true about the group?**

#	a	b	c	d
a	c	d	b	a
b	d	c	a	b
c	b	a	d	c
d	a	b	c	d

     I. The identity element of the group is d.
     II. The inverse of c is c.
     III. The operation # is commutative.

    a. I
    b. III
    c. I, III
    d. I, II, III

28. **If the square of twice the sum of x and three is equal to the product of twenty-four and x, which of these is a possible value of x?**

    a. $6 + 3\sqrt{2}$
    b. $\dfrac{3}{2}$
    c. $-3i$
    d. -3

29. **Given that x is a prime number and the greatest common factor of x and y is greater than 1, compare the two quantities.**

    Quantity A   Quantity B
    y the least common multiple of x and y

    a. Quantity A is greater.
    b. Quantity B is greater.
    c. The two quantities are the same.
    d. The relationship cannot be determined from the given information.

30. **If a, b, and c are even integers and $3a^2 + 9b^3 = c$, which of these is the largest number which must be factor of c?**

    a. 2
    b. 3
    c. 6
    d. 12

31. Which of these relationships represent y as a function of x?

a. $x = y^2$

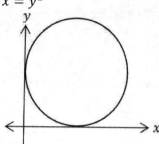

c. $y = [\![x]\!]$

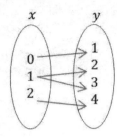

b.

d.

32. Express the area of the given triangle as a function of x.

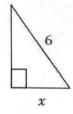

a. $A(x) = 3x$

b. $A(x) = \dfrac{x\sqrt{36-x^2}}{2}$

c. $A(x) = \dfrac{x^2}{2}$

d. $A(x) = 18 - \dfrac{x^2}{2}$

33. Find $[g \circ f]x$ when $f(x) = 2x + 4$ and $g(x) = x^2 - 3x + 2$.

a. $4x^2 + 10x + 6$

b. $2x^2 - 6x + 8$

c. $4x^2 + 13x + 18$

d. $2x^2 - 3x + 6$

34. Given the partial table of values for $f(x)$ and $g(x)$, find $f(g(-4))$. (Assume that $f(x)$ and $g(x)$ are the simplest polynomials that fit the data.)

x	$f(x)$	$g(x)$
-2	8	1
-1	2	3
0	0	5
1	2	7
2	8	9

a. 69
b. 31
c. 18
d. -3

35. If $f(x)$ and $g(x)$ are inverse functions, which of these is the value of x when $f(g(x)) = 4$?

    a. -4

    b. $\frac{1}{4}$

    c. 2

    d. 4

36. Determine which pair of equations are NOT inverses.

    a. $y = x + 6;\ y = x - 6$

    b. $y = 2x + 3;\ y = 2x - 3$

    c. $y = \frac{2x+3}{x-1};\ y = \frac{x+3}{x-2}$

    d. $y = \frac{x-1}{2};\ y = 2x + 1$

37. Which of these statements is (are) true for function $g(x)$?

$$g(x) = \begin{cases} 2x - 1 & x \geq 2 \\ -x + 3 & x < 2 \end{cases}$$

    I. $g(3) = 0$

    II. The graph of $g(x)$ is discontinuous at $x = 2$.

    III. The range of $g(x)$ is all real numbers.

    a. II

    b. III

    c. I, II

    d. II, III

38. Which of the following piecewise functions can describe the graph below?

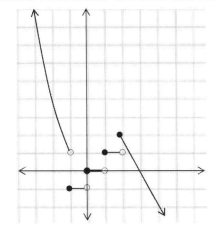

    a. $f(x) = \begin{cases} x^2 & x < -1 \\ [\![x]\!] & -1 \leq x < 2 \\ -2x + 6 & x \geq 2 \end{cases}$
    c. $f(x) = \begin{cases} (x+1)^2 & x < -1 \\ [\![x]\!] + 1 & -1 \leq x < 2 \\ -2x + 6 & x \geq 2 \end{cases}$

    b. $f(x) = \begin{cases} x^2 & x \leq -1 \\ [\![x]\!] & -1 \leq x \leq 2 \\ -2x + 6 & x > 2 \end{cases}$
    d. $f(x) = \begin{cases} (x+1)^2 & x < -1 \\ [\![x - 1]\!] & -1 \leq x < 2 \\ -2x + 6 & x \geq 2 \end{cases}$

39. Which of the following could be the graph of $y = a(x + b)(x + c)^2$ if $a > 0$?

a.

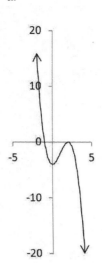

b.

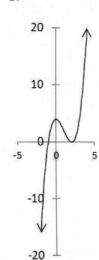

c.

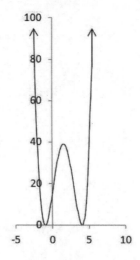

d.

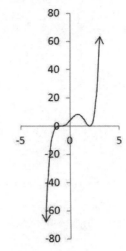

40. A school is selling tickets to its production of *Annie Get Your Gun*. Student tickets cost $3 each, and non-student tickets are $5 each. In order to offset the costs of the production, the school must earn at least $300 in ticket sales. Which graph shows the number of tickets the school must sell to offset production costs?

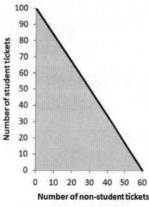

a.

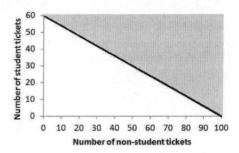

c.

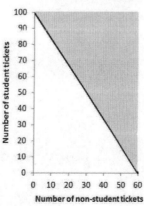

b.

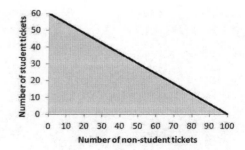

d.

41. Which of these is the equation graphed below?

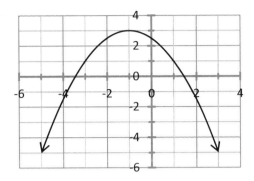

a. $y = -2x^2 - 4x + 1$
b. $y = -x^2 - 2x + 5$
c. $y = -x^2 - 2x + 2$
d. $y = -\frac{1}{2}x^2 - x + \frac{5}{2}$

42. Solve $7x^2 + 6x = -2$.

a. $x = \frac{-3 \pm \sqrt{23}}{7}$
b. $x = \pm i\sqrt{5}$
c. $x = \pm \frac{2i\sqrt{2}}{7}$
d. $x = \frac{-3 \pm i\sqrt{5}}{7}$

43. Solve the system of equations.

$$3x + 4y = 2$$
$$2x + 6y = -2$$

a. $\left(0, \frac{1}{2}\right)$
b. $\left(\frac{2}{5}, \frac{1}{5}\right)$
c. $(2, -1)$
d. $\left(-1, \frac{5}{4}\right)$

44. Which system of linear inequalities has no solution?

a. $x - y < 3$ and $x - y \geq -3$
b. $y \leq 6 - 2x$ and $\frac{1}{3}y + \frac{2}{3}x \geq 2$
c. $6x + 2y \leq 12$ and $3x \geq 8 - y$
d. $x + 4y \leq -8$ and $y + 4x > -8$

45. The cost of admission to a theme park is shown below.

	Under age 10	Ages 10-65	Over age 65
	$15	$25	$20

Yesterday, the theme park sold 810 tickets and earned $14,500. There were twice as many children under 10 at the park as there were other visitors. If x, y, and z represent the number of $15, $25, and $20 tickets sold, respectively, which of the following can be used to find how many of each sold?

a. $\begin{bmatrix} 1 & 1 & 1 \\ 15 & 25 & 20 \\ 1 & -2 & -2 \end{bmatrix} \begin{bmatrix} x \\ y \\ z \end{bmatrix} = \begin{bmatrix} 810 \\ 14,500 \\ 0 \end{bmatrix}$

b. $\begin{bmatrix} 1 & 1 & 1 \\ 15 & 25 & 20 \\ 1 & -2 & -2 \end{bmatrix} \begin{bmatrix} 810 \\ 14,500 \\ 0 \end{bmatrix} = \begin{bmatrix} x \\ y \\ z \end{bmatrix}$

c. $\begin{bmatrix} 1 & 15 & 1 \\ 1 & 25 & -2 \\ 1 & 20 & -2 \end{bmatrix} \begin{bmatrix} x \\ y \\ z \end{bmatrix} = \begin{bmatrix} 810 \\ 14,500 \\ 0 \end{bmatrix}$

d. $\begin{bmatrix} 1 & 15 & 1 \\ 1 & 25 & -2 \\ 1 & 20 & -2 \end{bmatrix} \begin{bmatrix} 810 \\ 14,500 \\ 0 \end{bmatrix} = \begin{bmatrix} x \\ y \\ z \end{bmatrix}$

46. Solve the system of equations.

$$2x - 4y + z = 10$$
$$-3x + 2y - 4z = -7$$
$$x + y - 3z = -1$$

a. $(-1, -3, 0)$
b. $(1, -2, 0)$
c. $(-\frac{3}{4}, -\frac{21}{8}, -1)$
d. No solution

47. Solve $x^4 + 64 = 20x^2$.

a. $x = \{2, 4\}$
b. $x = \{-4, -2, 2, 4\}$
c. $x = \{2i, 4i\}$
d. $x = \{-4i, -2i, 2i, 4i\}$

48. Solve $3x^3y^2 - 45x^2y = 15x^3y - 9x^2y^2$ for x and y.

a. $x = \{0, -3\}, y = \{0, 5\}$
b. $x = \{0\}, y = \{0\}$
c. $x = \{0, -3\}, y = \{0\}$
d. $x = \{0\}, y = \{0, 5\}$

49. Which of these statements is true for functions $f(x)$, $g(x)$, and $h(x)$?

$$f(x) = 2x - 2$$
$$g(x) = 2x^2 - 2$$
$$h(x) = 2x^3 - 2$$

a. The degree of each polynomial function is 2.
b. The leading coefficient of each function is –2.
c. Each function has exactly one real zero at $x = 1$.
d. None of these is true for functions $f(x)$, $g(x)$, and $h(x)$.

50. Which of these can be modeled by a quadratic function?

a. The path of a sound wave
b. The path of a bullet
c. The distance an object travels over time when the rate is constant
d. Radioactive decay

51. Which of these is equivalent to $\log_y 256$ if $2\log_4 y + \log_4 16 = 3$?

a. 16
b. 8
c. 4
d. 2

52. Simplify $\dfrac{(x^2 y)(2xy^{-2})^3}{16x^5 y^2} + \dfrac{3}{xy}$

a. $\dfrac{3x + 24y^6}{8xy^7}$

b. $\dfrac{x + 6y^6}{2xy^7}$

c. $\dfrac{x + 24y^5}{8xy^6}$

d. $\dfrac{x + 6y^5}{2xy^6}$

53. Given: $f(x) = 10^x$. If $f(x) = 5$, which of these approximates x?

a. 100,000
b. 0.00001
c. 0.7
d. 1.6

54. Which of these statements is NOT necessarily true when $f(x) = \log_b x$ and $b > 1$?

a. The x-intercept of the graph of $f(x)$ is 1.
b. The graph of $f(x)$ passes through $(b, 1)$
c. $f(x) < 0$ when $x < 1$
d. If $g(x) = b^x$, the graph of $f(x)$ is symmetric to the graph of $g(x)$ with respect to $y = x$.

55. Which of these could be the equation of the function graphed below?

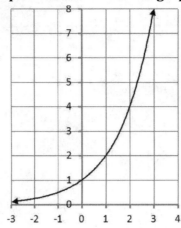

 a. $f(x) = x^2$
 b. $f(x) = \sqrt{x}$
 c. $f(x) = 2^x$
 d. $f(x) = \log_2 x$

56. A colony of *Escherichia coli* is inoculated from a Petri dish into a test tube containing 50 mL of nutrient broth. The test tube is placed in a 37°C incubator/shaker; after one hour, the number of bacteria in the test tube is determined to be 8×10^6. Given that the doubling time of *E. coli* is 20 minutes with agitation at 37°C, approximately how many bacteria should the test tube contain after eight hours of growth?

 a. 2.56×10^8
 b. 2.05×10^9
 c. 1.7×10^{14}
 d. 1.7×10^{13}

57. The strength of an aqueous acid solution is measured by pH. $\text{pH} = -\log_{10}[\text{H}^+]$, where $[\text{H}^+]$ is the molar concentration of hydronium ions in the solution. A solution is acidic if its pH is less than 7. The lower the pH, the stronger the acid; for example, gastric acid, which has a pH of about 1, is a much stronger acid than urine, which has a pH of about 6. How many times stronger is an acid with a pH of 3 than an acid with pH of 4?

 a. 2
 b. 10
 c. 100
 d. 1,000

58. Simplify $\sqrt{\dfrac{-28x^6}{27y^5}}$.

 a. $\dfrac{2x^3 i\sqrt{21y}}{9y^3}$

 b. $\dfrac{2x^3 i\sqrt{21y}}{27y^4}$

 c. $\dfrac{-2x^3 \sqrt{21y}}{9y^3}$

 d. $\dfrac{12x^3 yi\sqrt{7}}{27y^2}$

86

59. **Which of these does NOT have a solution set of $-1 \leq x \leq 1$?**

a. $-4 \leq 2 + 3(x - 1) \leq 2$

b. $-2x^2 + 2 \geq x^2 - 1$

c. $\frac{11 - |3x|}{7} \geq 2$

d. $3|2x| + 4 \leq 10$

60. **Solve $2 - \sqrt{x} = \sqrt{x - 20}$.**

a. $x = 6$

b. $x = 36$

c. $x = 144$

d. No solution

61. **Solve $\frac{x-2}{x-1} = \frac{x-1}{x+1} + \frac{2}{x-1}$.**

a. $x = 2$

b. $x = -5$

c. $x = 1$

d. No solution

62. **Which of these equations is represented by the graph below?**

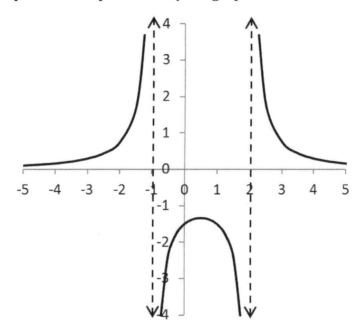

a. $y = \dfrac{3}{x^2 - x - 2}$

b. $y = \dfrac{3x+3}{x^2 - x - 2}$

c. $y = \dfrac{1}{x+1} + \dfrac{1}{x-2}$

d. None of these

63. Which of the graphs shown represents $f(x) = -2|-x + 4| - 1$?

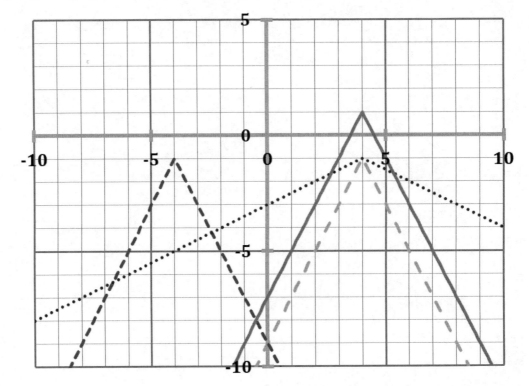

a. ▬ ▬

b. ▬▬▬

c. ▬▬▬▬

d. ••••••

64. Which of these functions includes 1 as an element of the domain and 2 as an element of the range?

a. $y = \frac{1}{x-1} + 1$

b. $y = -\sqrt{x + 2} - 1$

c. $y = |x + 2| - 3$

d. $y = \begin{cases} x & x < -1 \\ -x - 3 & x \geq -1 \end{cases}$

65. Which of the following statements is (are) true when $f(x) = \frac{x^2 - x - 6}{x^3 + 2x^2 - x - 2}$?

I. The graph $f(x)$ has vertical asymptotes at $x = -2$, $x = -1$, and $x = 1$.

II. The x- and y-intercepts of the graph of $f(x)$ are both 3.

a. I

b. II

c. I and II

d. Neither statement is true.

66. If 1 inch on a map represents 60 feet, how many yards apart are two points if the distance between the points on the map is 10 inches?

    a. 1,800
    b. 600
    c. 200
    d. 2

67. In the 1600s, Galileo Galilei studied the motion of pendulums and discovered that the period of a pendulum, the time it takes to complete one full swing, is a function of the square root of the length of its string: $2\pi\sqrt{\frac{L}{g}}$, where L is the length of the string and g is the acceleration due to gravity.

Consider two pendulums released from the same pivot point and at the same angle, $\theta - 30°$. Pendulum 1 has a mass of 100 g, while Pendulum 2 has a mass of 200 g. If Pendulum 1 has a period four times the period of Pendulum 2, what is true of the lengths of the pendulums' strings?

    a. The length of Pendulum 1's string is four times the length of Pendulum 2's string.
    b. The length of Pendulum 1's string is eight times the length of Pendulum 2's string.
    c. The length of Pendulum 1's string is sixteen times the length of Pendulum 2's string.
    d. The length of Pendulum 1's string is less than the length of Pendulum 2's string.

68. At today's visit to her doctor, Josephine was prescribed a liquid medication with instructions to take 25 cc's every four hours. She filled the prescription on her way to work, but when it came time to take the medicine, she realized that the pharmacist did not include a measuring cup. Josephine estimated that the plastic spoon in her desk drawer was about the same size as a teaspoon and decided to use it to measure the approximate dosage. She recalled that one cubic centimeter (cc) is equal to one milliliter (mL) but was not sure how many milliliters were in a teaspoon. So, she noted that a two-liter bottle of soda contains about the same amount as a half-gallon container of milk and applied her knowledge of the customary system of measurement to determine how many teaspoons of medicine to take. Which of these calculations might she have used to approximate her dosage?

    a. $25 \times \frac{1}{1,000} \times \frac{2}{0.5} \times 16 \times 48$
    b. $25 \times \frac{1}{100} \times \frac{0.5}{2} \times 16 \times 4 \times 12$
    c. $\frac{1,000}{25} \times \frac{0.5}{2} \times 16 \times 4 \times 12$
    d. $\frac{25}{1,000} \times \frac{1}{4} \times 16 \times 48$

69. Roxana walks x meters west and $x + 20$ meters south to get to her friend's house. On a neighborhood map which has a scale of 1 cm: 10 m, the distance between Roxana's house and her friend's house is 10 cm. How far did Roxana walk to her friend's house?

   a. 60 m
   b. 80 m
   c. 100 m
   d. 140 m

70. For $\triangle ABC$, what is $\overline{AB}$?

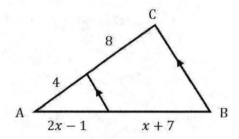

   a. 3
   b. 10
   c. 12
   d. 15

71. To test the accuracy and precision of two scales, a student repeatedly measured the mass of a 10g standard and recorded these results.

	Trial 1	Trial 2	Trial 3	Trial 4
Scale 1	9.99 g	9.98 g	10.02g	10.01g
Scale 2	10.206 g	10.209 g	10.210 g	10.208 g

Which of these conclusions about the scales is true?

   a. Scale 1 has an average percent error of 0.15%, and Scale 2 has an average percent error of 2.08%. Scale 1 is more accurate and precise than Scale 2.
   b. Scale 1 has an average percent error of 0.15%, and Scale 2 has an average percent error of 2.08%. Scale 1 is more accurate than Scale 2; however, Scale 2 is more precise.
   c. Scale 1 has an average percent error of 0%, and Scale 2 has an average percent error of 2.08%. Scale 1 is more accurate and precise than Scale 2.
   d. Scale 1 has an average percent error of 0%, and Scale 2 has an average percent error of 2.08%. Scale 1 is more accurate than Scale 2; however, Scale 2 is more precise.

72. A developer decides to build a fence around a neighborhood park, which is positioned on a rectangular lot. Rather than fencing along the lot line, he fences x feet from each of the lot's boundaries. By fencing a rectangular space 141 yd^2 smaller than the lot, the developer saves $432 in fencing materials, which cost $12 per linear foot. How much does he spend?

   a. $160
   b. $456
   c. $3,168
   d. The answer cannot be determined from the given information.

73. Natasha designs a square pyramidal tent for her children. Each of the sides of the square base measures x ft, and the tent's height is h feet. If Natasha were to increase by 1 ft the length of each side of the base, how much more interior space would the tent have?

a. $\frac{h(x^2+2x+1)}{3}$ ft^3

b. $\frac{h(2x+1)}{3}$ ft^3

c. $\frac{x^2h+3}{3}$ ft^3

d. 1 ft^3

74. A rainbow pattern is designed from semi-circles as shown below.

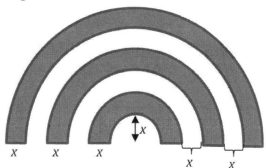

X X X X X

Which of the following gives the area A of the shaded region as a function of x?

a. $A = \frac{21x^2\pi}{2}$

b. $A = 21x^2\pi$

c. $A = 42x^2\pi$

d. $A = 82x^2\pi$

75. Categorize the following statements as axioms of Euclidean, hyperbolic, or elliptical geometry.

I. If a point is not on a given line, exactly one line parallel to the given line can be drawn through the point.

II. If a point is not on a given line, an infinite number of lines parallel to the given line can be drawn through the point.

III. If a point is not on a given line, no lines parallel to the given line can be drawn through the point.

a.

Statement I	Elliptical geometry
Statement II	Euclidean geometry
Statement III	Hyperbolic geometry

b.

Statement I	Euclidean geometry
Statement II	Hyperbolic geometry
Statement III	Elliptical geometry

c.

Statement I	Hyperbolic geometry
Statement II	Elliptical geometry
Statement III	Euclidean geometry

d.

Statement I	Elliptical geometry
Statement II	Hyperbolic geometry
Statement III	Euclidean geometry

76. A circle is inscribed inside quadrilateral $ABCD$. $\overline{CD}$ is bisected by the point at which it is tangent to the circle. If $\overline{AB} = 14, \overline{BC} = 10, \overline{CD} = 8$, then

a. $\overline{AD} = 11$

b. $\overline{AD} = 2\sqrt{34}$

c. $\overline{AD} = 12$

d. $\overline{AD} = 17.5$

77. As shown below, four congruent isosceles trapezoids are positioned such that they form an arch. Find x for the indicated angle.

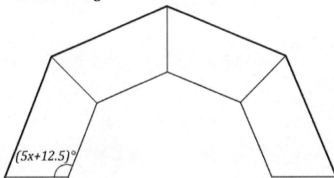

$(5x+12.5)°$

a. $x = 11$

b. $x = 20$

c. $x = 24.5$

d. The value of x cannot be determined from the information given.

78. Which of the following expressions gives the area A of the triangle below as a function of sides a and b?

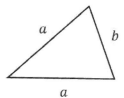

a. $\dfrac{2a^2-b^2}{4}$

b. $\dfrac{ab-a^2}{2}$

c. $\dfrac{b\sqrt{a^2-b^2}}{2}$

d. $\dfrac{b\sqrt{4a^2-b^2}}{4}$

79. Given the figure and the following information, find DE to the nearest tenth.

$\overline{AD}$ is an altitude of $\triangle ABC$
$\overline{DE}$ is an altitude of triangle $\triangle ADC$

$$\overline{BD} \cong \overline{DC}$$

$\overline{BC} = 24; \overline{AD} = 5$

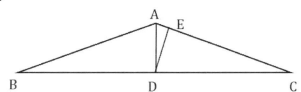

a. 4.2
b. 4.6
c. 4.9
d. 5.4

80. A cube inscribed in a sphere has a volume of 64 cubic units. What is the volume of the sphere in cubic units?

a. $4\pi\sqrt{3}$
b. $8\pi\sqrt{3}$
c. $32\pi\sqrt{3}$
d. $256\pi\sqrt{3}$

Refer to the following for questions 81 - 82:

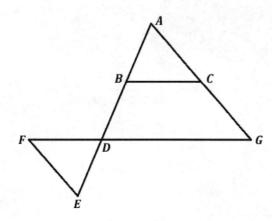

Statement	Reason
1. $\overline{BC} \parallel \overline{FG}$	Given
2.	
3. $\overline{FD} \cong \overline{BC}$	Given
4. $\overline{AB} \cong \overline{DE}$	Given
5. $\triangle ABC \cong \triangle EDF$	_____
6. _____	
7. $\overline{FE} \parallel \overline{AG}$	

Given: $\overline{BC} \parallel \overline{FG}$; $\overline{FD} \cong \overline{BC}$; $\overline{AB} \cong \overline{DE}$

Prove: $\overline{FE} \parallel \overline{AG}$

81. Which of the following justifies step 5 in the proof?
   a.   AAS
   b.   SSS
   c.   ASA
   d.   SAS

82. Step 6 in the proof should contain which of the following statements?
   a. $\angle BAC \cong \angle DEF$
   b. $\angle ABC \cong \angle EDF$
   c. $\angle ACB \cong \angle EFD$
   d. $\angle GDA \cong \angle EDF$

83. Which of these is NOT a net of a cube?
a.   b.   c.   d.

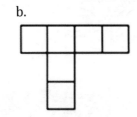
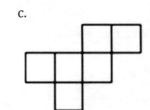
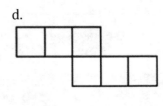

84. Identify the cross-section polygon formed by a plane containing the given points on the cube.

a. Rectangle
b. Trapezoid
c. Pentagon
d. Hexagon

85. Which of these represents the equation of a sphere which is centered in the xyz-space at the point $(1, 0, -2)$ and which has a volume of 36π cubic units?

a. $x^2 + y^2 + z^2 - 2x + 4z = 4$
b. $x^2 + y^2 + z^2 + 2x - 4z = 4$
c. $x^2 + y^2 + z^2 - 2x + 4z = -2$
d. $x^2 + y^2 + z^2 + 2x - 4z = 2$

86. A triangle has vertices $(0, 0, 0)$, $(0, 0, 4)$, and $(0, 3, 0)$ in the xyz-space. In cubic units, what is the difference in the volume of the solid formed by rotating the triangle about the z-axis and the solid formed by rotating the triangle about the y-axis?

a. 0
b. 4π
c. 5π
d. 25

87. If the midpoint of a line segment graphed on the xy-coordinate plane is $(3, -1)$ and the slope of the line segment is -2, which of these is a possible endpoint of the line segment?

a. $(-1, 1)$
b. $(0, -5)$
c. $(7, 1)$
d. $(5, -5)$

88. The vertices of a polygon are $(2, 3)$, $(8, 1)$, $(6, -5)$, and $(0, -3)$. Which of the following describes the polygon most specifically?

a. Parallelogram
b. Rhombus
c. Rectangle
d. Square

89. What is the radius of the circle defined by the equation $x^2 + y^2 - 10x + 8y + 29 = 0$?

a. $2\sqrt{3}$
b. $2\sqrt{5}$
c. $\sqrt{29}$
d. 12

90. Which of these describes the graph of the equation $2x^2 - 3y^2 - 12x + 6y - 15 = 0$?

   a. Circular
   b. Elliptical
   c. Parabolic
   d. Hyperbolic

91. The graph of $f(x)$ is a parabola with a focus of (a, b) and a directrix of $y = -b$, and $g(x)$ represents a transformation of $f(x)$. If the vertex of the graph of $g(x)$ is $(a, 0)$, which of these is a possible equation for $g(x)$ for nonzero integers a and b?

   a. $g(x) = f(x) + b$
   b. $g(x) = -f(x)$
   c. $g(x) = f(x + a)$
   d. $g(x) = f(x - a) + b$

92. A triangle with vertices $A(-4, 2)$, $B(-1, 3)$, and $C(-5, 7)$ is reflected across $y = x + 2$ to give $\Delta A'B'C'$, which is subsequently reflected across the y-axis to give $\Delta A''B''C''$. Which of these statements is true?

   a. A 90° rotation of ΔABC about $(-2,0)$ gives $\Delta A''B''C''$.
   b. A reflection of ΔABC about the x-axis gives $\Delta A''B''C''$.
   c. A 270° rotation of ΔABC about $(0,2)$ gives $\Delta A''B''C''$.
   d. A translation of ΔABC two units down gives $\Delta A''B''C''$.

93. For which of these does a rotation of 120° about the center of the polygon map the polygon onto itself?

   a. Square
   b. Regular hexagon
   c. Regular octagon
   d. Regular decagon

94. Line segment $\overline{PQ}$ has endpoints (a, b) and (c, b). If $\overline{P'Q'}$ is the translation of $\overline{PQ}$ along a diagonal line such that P' is located at point (c, d), what is the area of quadrilateral $PP'Q'Q$?

   a. $|a - c| \times |b - d|$
   b. $|a - b| \times |c - d|$
   c. $|a - d| \times |b - c|$
   d. $(a - c)^2$

95. For the right triangle below, where $a \neq b$, which of the following is a true statement of equality?

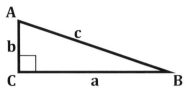

a. $\tan B = \frac{a}{b}$

b. $\cos B = \frac{a\sqrt{a^2+b^2}}{a^2+b^2}$

c. $\sec B = \frac{\sqrt{a^2+b^2}}{b}$

d. $\csc B = \frac{a^2+b^2}{b}$

96. A man looks out of a window of a tall building at a 45° angle of depression and sees his car in the parking lot. When he turns his gaze downward to a 60° angle of depression, he sees his wife's car. If his car is parked 60 feet from his wife's car, about how far from the building did his wife park her car?

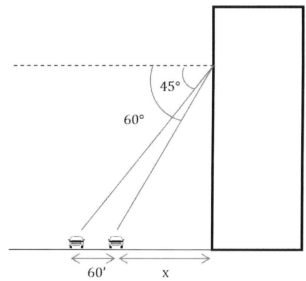

a. 163 feet
b. 122 feet
c. 82 feet
d. 60 feet

97. What is the exact value of $\tan\left(-\frac{2\pi}{3}\right)$?

a. $\sqrt{3}$

b. $-\sqrt{3}$

c. $\frac{\sqrt{3}}{3}$

d. 1

98. If $\sin \theta = \frac{1}{2}$ when $\frac{\pi}{2} < \theta < \pi$, what is the value of θ?

   a. $\frac{\pi}{6}$

   b. $\frac{\pi}{3}$

   c. $\frac{2\pi}{3}$

   d. $\frac{5\pi}{6}$

99. Which of the following expressions is equal to $\cos \theta \cot \theta$?

   a. $\sin \theta$
   b. $\sec \theta \tan \theta$
   c. $\csc \theta - \sin \theta$
   d. $\sec \theta - \sin \theta$

100. Solve $\sec^2 \theta = 2 \tan \theta$ for $0 < \theta \le 2\pi$.

   a. $\theta = \frac{\pi}{6}$ or $\frac{7\pi}{6}$

   b. $\theta = \frac{\pi}{4}$ or $\frac{5\pi}{4}$

   c. $\theta = \frac{3\pi}{4}$ or $\frac{7\pi}{4}$

   d. There is no solution to the equation.

101. A car is driving along the highway at a constant speed when it runs over a pebble, which becomes lodged in one of the tire's treads. If this graph represents the height h of the pebble above the road in inches as a function of time t in seconds, which of these statements is true?

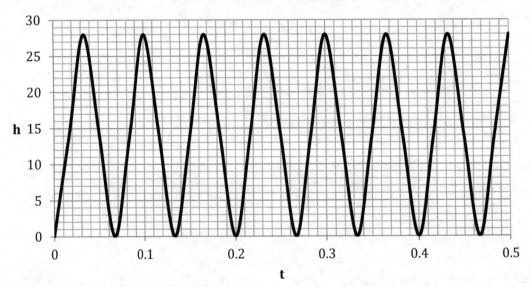

   a. The outer radius of the tire is 14 inches, and the tire rotates 900 times per minute.
   b. The outer radius of the tire is 28 inches, and the tire rotates 900 times per minute.
   c. The outer radius of the tire is 14 inches, and the tire rotates 120 times per minute.
   d. The outer radius of the tire is 28 inches, and the tire rotates 120 times per minute.

Refer to the following for questions 102 - 103:

Below are graphed functions $f(x) = a_1 \sin(b_1 x)$ and $g(x) = a_2 \cos(b_2 x)$; a_1 and a_2 are integers, and b_1 and b_2 are positive rational numbers.

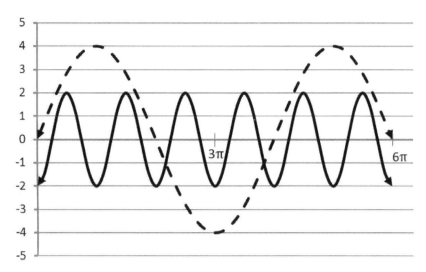

102. Which of the following statements is true?
- a. The graph of $f(x)$ is represented by a solid line.
- b. The amplitude of the graph of $g(x)$ is 4.
- c. $0 < b_1 < 1$
- d. $b_2 = \pi$

103. Which of the following statements is true?
- a. $0 < a_2 < a_1$
- b. $a_2 < 0 < a_1$
- c. $0 < a_1 < a_2$
- d. $a_2 < a_1 < 0$

104. A weight suspended on a spring is at its equilibrium point five inches above the top of a table. When the weight is pulled down two inches, it bounces above the equilibrium point and returns to the point from which it was released in one second. Which of these can be used to model the weight's height h above the table as a function of time t in seconds?
- a. $h = -2\cos(2\pi t) + 5$
- b. $h = 5\sin(\pi t) - 2$
- c. $h = -2\sin(2\pi t) + 5$
- d. $h = -2\cos(0.5\pi t) + 3$

105. Evaluate $\lim\limits_{x \to -3} \dfrac{x^3 + 3x^2 - x - 3}{x^2 - 9}$.
- a. 0
- b. $\dfrac{1}{3}$
- c. $-\dfrac{4}{3}$
- d. ∞

106. Evaluate $\lim\limits_{x\to\infty} \frac{x^2+2x-3}{2x^2+1}$.

    a. 0

    b. $\frac{1}{2}$

    c. -3

    d. ∞

107. Evaluate $\lim\limits_{x\to3^+} \frac{|x-3|}{3-x}$.

    a. 0

    b. -1

    c. 1

    d. ∞

108. If $f(x) = \frac{1}{4}x^2 - 3$**, find the slope of the line tangent to graph of** $f(x)$ **at** $x = 2$.

    a. -2

    b. 0

    c. 1

    d. 4

109. If $f(x) = 2x^3 - 3x^2 + 4$**, what is** $\lim\limits_{h\to0} \frac{f(2+h)-f(2)}{h}$?

    a. -4

    b. 4

    c. 8

    d. 12

110. Find the derivative of $f(x) = e^{3x^2-1}$.

    a. $6xe^{6x}$

    b. e^{3x^2-1}

    c. $(3x^2 - 1)e^{3x^2-2}$

    d. $6xe^{3x^2-1}$

111. Find the derivative of $f(x) = \ln(2x + 1)$.

    a. $\frac{1}{2x+1}$

    b. $2e^{2x+1}$

    c. $\frac{2}{2x+1}$

    d. $\frac{1}{2}$

112. For functions $f(x)$, $g(x)$, and $h(x)$, determine the limit of the function as x approaches 2 and the continuity of the function at $x = 2$ given:

$$\lim_{x \to 2+} f(x) = 4 \qquad \lim_{x \to 2+} g(x) = 2 \qquad \lim_{x \to 2+} h(x) = 2$$

$$\lim_{x \to 2-} f(x) = 2 \qquad \lim_{x \to 2-} g(x) = 2 \qquad \lim_{x \to 2-} h(x) = 2$$

$$f(2) = 2 \qquad\qquad g(2) = 4 \qquad\qquad h(2) = 2$$

a. $\begin{cases} \lim_{x \to 2} f(x) \, DNE & \text{The function } f(x) \text{ is discontinuous at 2} \\ \lim_{x \to 2} g(x) = 2 & \text{The function } g(x) \text{ is discontinuous at 2} \\ \lim_{x \to 2} h(x) = 2 & \text{The function } h(x) \text{ is continuous at 2} \end{cases}$

b. $\begin{cases} \lim_{x \to 2} f(x) \, DNE & \text{The function } f(x) \text{ is continuous at 2} \\ \lim_{x \to 2} g(x) \, DNE & \text{The function } g(x) \text{ is continuous at 2} \\ \lim_{x \to 2} h(x) = 2 & \text{The function } h(x) \text{ is continuous at 2} \end{cases}$

c. $\begin{cases} \lim_{x \to 2} f(x) = 2 & \text{The function } f(x) \text{ is continuous at 2} \\ \lim_{x \to 2} g(x) = 2 & \text{The function } g(x) \text{ is discontinuous at 2} \\ \lim_{x \to 2} h(x) = 2 & \text{The function } h(x) \text{ is continuous at 2} \end{cases}$

d. $\begin{cases} \lim_{x \to 2} f(x) = 2 & \text{The function } f(x) \text{ is discontinuous at 2} \\ \lim_{x \to 2} g(x) = 2 & \text{The function } g(x) \text{ is discontinuous at 2} \\ \lim_{x \to 2} h(x) = 2 & \text{The function } h(x) \text{ is continuous at 2} \end{cases}$

113. Find $f''(x)$ if $f(x) = 2x^4 - 4x^3 + 2x^2 - x + 1$.

a. $24x^2 - 24x + 4$
b. $8x^3 - 12x^2 + 4x - 1$
c. $32x^2 - 36x^2 + 8$
d. $\frac{2}{5}x^5 - x^4 + \frac{2}{3}x^3 - \frac{1}{2}x^2 + x + c$

114. If $f(x) = 4x^3 - x^2 - 4x + 2$, which of the following statements is(are) true of its graph?

    I. The point $\left(-\frac{1}{2}, 3\frac{1}{4}\right)$ is a relative maximum.

    II. The graph of f is concave upward on the interval $\left(-\infty, \frac{1}{2}\right)$.

a. I
b. II
c. I and II
d. Neither I nor II

115. Suppose the path of a baseball hit straight up from three feet above the ground is modeled by the first quadrant graph of the function $h = -16t^2 + 50t + 3$, where t is the flight time of the ball in seconds and h is the height of the ball in feet. What is the velocity of the ball two seconds after it is hit?

a. 39 ft/s upward
b. 19.5 ft/s upward
c. 19.5 ft/s downward
d. 14 ft/s downward

116. A manufacturer wishes to produce a cylindrical can which can hold up to 0.5 L of liquid. To the nearest tenth, what is the radius of the can which requires the least amount of material to make?

    a. 2.8 cm
    b. 4.3 cm
    c. 5.0 cm
    d. 9.2 cm

117. To the nearest hundredth, what is the area in square units under the curve $f(x) = \frac{1}{x}$ on $[1, 2]$?

    a. 0.50
    b. 0.69
    c. 1.30
    d. 1.50

118. Approximate the area A under the curve by using a Riemann sum with $\Delta x = 1$.

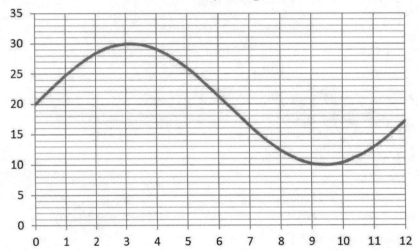

    a. $209 < A < 211$
    b. $230 < A < 235$
    c. $238 < A < 241$
    d. $246 < A < 250$

119. Calculate $\int 3x^2 + 2x - 1\, dx$.

    a. $x^3 + x^2 - x + C$
    b. $6x^2 + 2$
    c. $\frac{3}{2}x^3 + 2x^2 - x + C$
    d. $6x^2 + 2 + C$

120. Calculate $\int 3x^2 e^{x^3}\, dx$

    a. $x^3 e^{x^3} + C$
    b. $e^{x^3} + C$
    c. $x^3 e^{\frac{x^4}{4}} + C$
    d. $\ln x^3 + C$

121. Find the area A of the finite region between the graphs of $y = -x + 2$ and $y = x^2 - 4$.

    a. 18

    b. $\dfrac{125}{6}$

    c. $\dfrac{45}{2}$

    d. 25

122. The velocity of a car which starts at position 0 at time 0 is given by the equation $v(t) = 12t - t^2$ for $0 \le t \le 12$. Find the position of the car when its acceleration is 0.

    a. 18

    b. 36

    c. 144

    d. 288

123. Which of these graphs is NOT representative of the data set shown below?

```
3|6799
4|23889            KEY
5|011157   2|123 = 21, 22, 23
6|00123
```

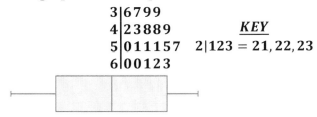

a.

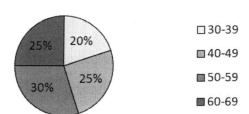

b.

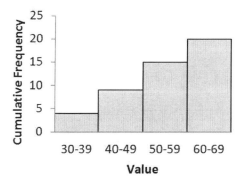

c.

    d.   All of these graphs represent the data set.

124. Which of these would best illustrate change over time?

a. Pie chart
b. Line graph
c. Box-and-whisker plot
d. Venn diagram

125. Which of these is the least biased sampling technique?

a. To assess his effectiveness in the classroom, a teacher distributes a teacher evaluation to all of his students. Responses are anonymous and voluntary.
b. To determine the average intelligence quotient (IQ) of students in her school of 2,000 students, a principal uses a random number generator to select 300 students by student identification number and has them participate in a standardized IQ test.
c. To determine which video game is most popular among his fellow eleventh graders at school, a student surveys all of the students in his English class.
d. Sixty percent of students at the school have a parent who is a member of the Parent-Teacher Association (PTA). To determine parent opinions regarding school improvement programs, the Parent-Teacher Association (PTA) requires submission of a survey response with membership dues.

126. Which of these tables properly displays the measures of central tendency that can be used for nominal, interval, and ordinal data?

a.

	Mean	Median	Mode
Nominal			X
Interval	X	X	X
Ordinal		X	X

b.

	Mean	Median	Mode
Nominal			X
Interval	X	X	X
Ordinal	X	X	X

c.

	Mean	Median	Mode
Nominal	X	X	X
Interval	X	X	X
Ordinal	X	X	X

d.

	Mean	Median	Mode
Nominal			X
Interval	X	X	
Ordinal	X	X	X

Refer to the following for questions 127 - 129:

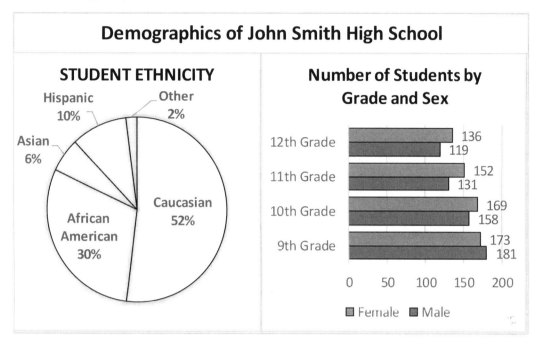

Demographics of John Smith High School

127. Which of these is the greatest quantity?
a. The average number of male students in the 11th and 12th grades
b. The number of Hispanic students at the school
c. The difference in the number of male and female students at the school
d. The difference in the number of 9th and 12th grade students at the school

128. Compare the two quantities.

Quantity A	Quantity B
The percentage of white students at the school, rounded to the nearest whole number	The percentage of female students at the school, rounded to the nearest whole number

a. Quantity A is greater.
b. Quantity B is greater.
c. The two quantities are the same.
d. The relationship cannot be determined from the given information.

129. An eleventh grader is chosen at random to represent the school at a conference. What is the approximate probability that the student is male?
a. 0.03
b. 0.11
c. 0.22
d. 0.46

Refer to the following for questions 130 - 132:

The box-and-whisker plot displays student test scores by class period.

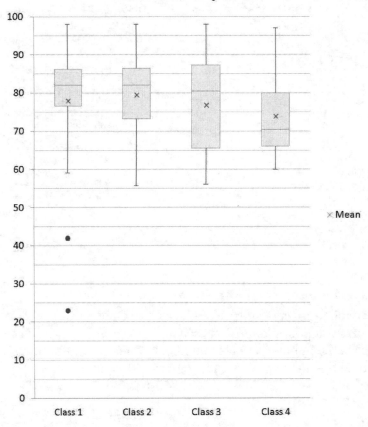

130. Which class has the greatest range of test scores?

    a.   Class 1
    b.   Class 2
    c.   Class 3
    d.   Class 4

131. What is the probability that a student chosen at random from Class 2 made above a 73 on this test?

    a.   0.25
    b.   0.5
    c.   0.6
    d.   0.75

132. Which of the following statements is true of the data?

    a.   The mean better reflects student performance in class 1 than the median.
    b.   The mean test score for class 1 and 2 is the same.
    c.   The median test score for class 1 and 2 is the same.
    d.   The median test score is above the mean for class 4.

133. In order to analyze the real estate market for two different zip codes within the city, a realtor examines the most recent 100 home sales in each zip code. She considered a house which sold within the first month of its listing to have a market time of one month; likewise, she considered a house to have a market time of two months if it sold after having been on the market for one month but by the end of the second month. Using this definition of market time, she determined the frequency of sales by the number of months on the market. The results are displayed below.

Which of the following is a true statement for these data?

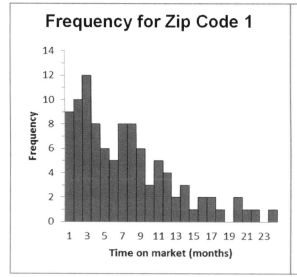 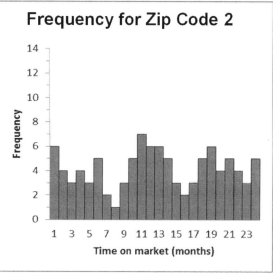

a. The median time a house spends on the market in Zip Code 1 is five months less than Zip Code 2

b. On average, a house spent seven months longer on the market in Zip Code 2 than in Zip Code 1.

c. The mode time on the market is higher for Zip Code 1 than for Zip Code 2.

d. The median time on the market is less than the mean time on the market for Zip Code 1.

134. Attending a summer camp are 12 six-year-olds, 15 seven-year-olds, 14 eight-year-olds, 12 nine-year-olds, and 10 ten-year-olds. If a camper is randomly selected to participate in a special event, what is the probability that he or she is at least eight years old?

a. $\frac{2}{9}$

b. $\frac{22}{63}$

c. $\frac{4}{7}$

d. $\frac{3}{7}$

135. A small company is divided into three departments as shown. Two individuals are chosen at random to attend a conference. What is the approximate probability that two women from the same department will be chosen?

	Department 1	Department 2	Department 3
Women	12	28	16
Men	18	14	15

a. 8.6%
b. 10.7%
c. 11.2%
d. 13.8%

136. A random sample of 90 students at an elementary school were asked these three questions:

Do you like carrots?
Do you like broccoli?
Do you like cauliflower?

The results of the survey are shown below. If these data are representative of the population of students at the school, which of these is most probable?

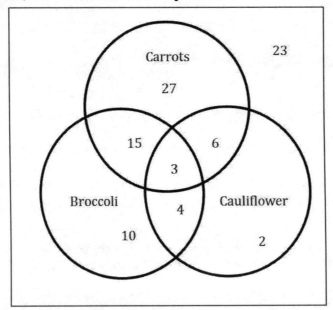

a. A student chosen at random likes broccoli.
b. If a student chosen at random likes carrots, they will also like at least one other vegetable.
c. If a student chosen at random likes cauliflower and broccoli, they will also like carrots.
d. A student chosen at random does not like carrots, broccoli, or cauliflower.

Refer to the following for questions 137 - 138:

Each day for 100 days, a student tossed a single misshapen coin three times in succession and recorded the number of times the coin landed on heads. The results of his experiment are shown below.

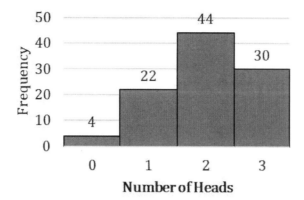

137. Given these experimental data, which of these approximates $P(\text{heads})$ for a single flip of this coin?

    a.   0.22
    b.   0.5
    c.   0.67
    d.   0.74

138. Which of these shows the graphs of the probability distributions from ten flips of this misshapen coin and ten flips of a fair coin?

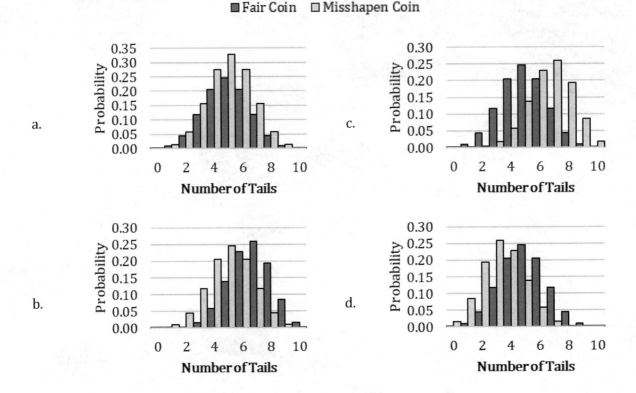

139. Which of these does NOT simulate randomly selecting a student from a group of 11 students?

    a.   Assigning each student a unique card value of A, 2, 3, 4, 5, 6, 7, 8, 9, 10, or J, removing queens and kings from a standard deck of 52 cards, shuffling the remaining cards, and drawing a single card from the deck

    b.   Assigning each student a unique number 0-10 and using a computer to randomly generate a number within that range

    c.   Assigning each student a unique number from 2 to 12; rolling two dice and finding the sum of the numbers on the dice

    d.   All of these can be used as a simulation of the event.

140. Gene P has three possible alleles, or gene forms, called *a*, *b* and *c*. Each individual carries two copies of Gene P, one of which is inherited from his or her mother and the other of which is inherited from his or her father. If the two copies of Gene P are of the same form, the individual is homozygous for that allele; otherwise, the individual is heterozygous. The following table represents genetic data from 500 individuals selected at random from the population.

		Allele 2		
		a	b	c
Allele 1	a	6	10	39
	b	11	21	79
	c	36	65	233

Using experimental probability, predict the number of individuals in a population of 100,000 who will be homozygous for either the a or b allele.

    a. 2,800
    b. 5,000
    c. 5,400
    d. 9,000

141. The intelligence quotients (IQs) of a randomly selected group of 300 people are normally distributed with a mean IQ of 100 and a standard deviation of 15. In a normal distribution, approximately 68% of values are within one standard deviation of the mean. About how many individuals from the selected group have IQs of at least 85?

    a. 96
    b. 200
    c. 216
    d. 252

142. How many different seven-digit telephone numbers can be created in which no digit repeats and in which zero cannot be the first digit?

    a. 5,040
    b. 35,280
    c. 544,320
    d. 3,265,920

143. A teacher wishes to divide her class of twenty students into four groups, each of which will have three boys and two girls. How many possible groups can she form?

    a. 248
    b. 6,160
    c. 73,920
    d. 95,040

144. In how many distinguishable ways can a family of five be seated at a circular table with five chairs if Tasha and Mac must be kept separated?

    a. 6
    b. 12
    c. 24
    d. 60

145. Which of these defines the recursive sequence $a_1 = -1, a_{n+1} = a_n + 2$ explicitly?

    a. $a_n = 2n - 3$
    b. $a_n = -n + 2$
    c. $a_n = n - 2$
    d. $a_n = -2n + 3$

146. What is the sum of the series $200 + 100 + 50 + 25 + \cdots$?

    a. 375
    b. 400
    c. 600
    d. The sum is infinite.

147. For vector $v = (4, 3)$ and vector $w = (-3, 4)$, find $2(v + w)$.

    a. $(2, 14)$
    b. $(14, -2)$
    c. $(1, 7)$
    d. $(7, -1)$

148. Simplify:

$$[2 \quad 0 \quad -5]\left(\begin{bmatrix} 4 \\ 2 \\ -1 \end{bmatrix} - \begin{bmatrix} 3 \\ 5 \\ -5 \end{bmatrix} \right)$$

    a. $[-18]$
    b. $\begin{bmatrix} 2 \\ 0 \\ -20 \end{bmatrix}$
    c. $[2 \quad 0 \quad -20]$
    d. $\begin{bmatrix} 2 & 0 & -5 \\ -6 & 0 & 15 \\ 8 & 0 & -20 \end{bmatrix}$

149. Consider three sets, of which one contains the set of even integers, one contains the factors of twelve, and one contains elements 1, 2, 4, and 9. If each set is assigned the name A, B, or C, and $A \cap B \subseteq B \cap C$, which of these must be set C?

    a. The set of even integers
    b. The set of factors of 12
    c. The set $\{1, 2, 4, 9\}$
    d. The answer cannot be determined from the given information.

150. Last year, Jenny tutored students in math, in chemistry, and for the ACT. She tutored ten students in math, eight students in chemistry, and seven students for the ACT. She tutored five students in both math and chemistry, and she tutored four students both in chemistry and for the ACT, and five students both in math and for the ACT. She tutored three students in all three subjects. How many students did Jenny tutor last year?

    a. 34
    b. 25
    c. 23
    d. 14

Answer Key and Explanations

1. C: One strategy is to consider a progression of polygons with fewer sides and look for a pattern in the number of the polygons' diagonals.

Polygon	Sides	Diagonals	Additional Diagonals
(triangle)	3	0	-
(square)	4	2	2
(pentagon)	5	5	3
(hexagon)	6	9	4

A quadrilateral has two more diagonals than a triangle, a pentagon has three more diagonals than a quadrilateral, and a hexagon has four more diagonals than a pentagon. Continue this pattern to find that a dodecagon has 54 diagonals.

2. B: The problem does not give any information about the size of the bracelet or the spacing between any of the charms. Nevertheless, creating a simple illustration which shows the order of the charms will help when approaching this problem. For example, the circle below represents the bracelet, and the dotted line between A and B represents the clasp. On the right, the line shows the stretched-out bracelet and possible positions of charms C, D, and E based on the parameters.

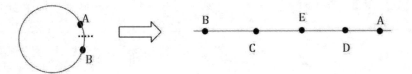

From the drawing above, it appears that statement I is true, but it is not necessarily so. The alternative drawing below also shows the charms ordered correctly, but the distance between B and E is now less than that between D and A.

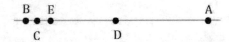

Statement II must be true: charm E must lie between B and D. Statement III must also be true: the distance between charms E and D must be less than that between C and A, which includes charms E and D in the space between them.

3. B: The population is approximately 36,000, so one-quarter of the population consists of about 9,000 individuals under age 35. A third of 9,000 is 3,000, the approximate number of students in

114

grades K-12. Since there are thirteen grades, there are about 230 students in each grade. So, the number of fourth graders is between 200 and 300.

4. A: The final sales price of the rug is:

$$1.08(0.7 \times \$296) = \$223.78 \text{ at Store A}$$
$$1.08(\$220 - \$10) = \$226.80 \text{ at Store B}$$
$$\$198 + \$35 = \$233 \text{ at Store C}$$

5. C: The expression representing the monthly charge for Company A is $\$25 + \$0.05m$, where m is the time in minutes spent talking on the phone. Set this expression equal to the monthly charge for Company B, which is $50. Solve for m to find the number of minutes for which the two companies charge the same amount:

$$\$25 + \$0.05m = \$50$$
$$\$0.05m = \$25$$
$$m = 500$$

Notice that the answer choices are given in hours, not in minutes. Since there are 60 minutes in an hour, $m = \frac{500}{60}$ hours $= 8\frac{1}{3}$ hours. One-third of an hour is 20 minutes, so $m = 8$ hours 20 minutes.

6. D: When the dress is marked down by 20%, the cost of the dress is 80% of its original price; thus, the reduced price of the dress can be written as $\frac{80}{100}x$, or $\frac{4}{5}x$, where x is the original price. When discounted an extra 25%, the dress costs 75% of the reduced price, or $\frac{75}{100}\left(\frac{4}{5}x\right)$, or $\frac{3}{4}\left(\frac{4}{5}x\right)$, which simplifies to $\frac{3}{5}x$. So the final price of the dress is three-fifths of the original price.

7. D: Since there are 100 cm in a meter, on a 1:100 scale drawing, each centimeter represents one meter. Therefore, an area of one square centimeter on the drawing represents one square meter in actuality. Since the area of the room in the scale drawing is 30 cm^2, the room's actual area is 30 m^2.

Another way to determine the area of the room is to write and solve an equation, such as this one: $l/100 \times w/100 = 30$ cm^2 , where l and w are the dimensions of the actual room

$$lw/10{,}000 = 30 \text{ cm}^2$$

$$\text{Area} = 300{,}000 \text{ cm}^2$$

Since this is not one of the answer choices, convert cm^2 to m^2:

$$300{,}000 \text{ cm}^2 \times \frac{1 \text{ m}}{100 \text{ cm}} \times \frac{1 \text{ m}}{100 \text{ cm}} = 30 \text{ m}^2.$$

8. C: When you have a ratio, you can find the fraction that each part of the ratio is of the whole by putting it over the sum of the parts. In other words, since the ratio of wages and benefits to other costs is 2: 3, the amount of money spent on wages and benefits is $\frac{2}{2+3} = \frac{2}{5}$ of total expenditures.

$$\frac{2}{5} \times \$130{,}000 = \$52{,}000$$

9. C: The height of the ball is a function of time, so the equation can be expressed as $f(t) = -18t^2 + 72t + 4$, and the average rate of change can be found by calculating $\frac{f(3)-f(0)}{3-0}$.

$$\frac{-18(3)^2 + 72(3) + 4 - [-18(0)^2 + 64(0) + 4]}{3} = \frac{-162 + 216 + 4 - (0 + 0 + 4)}{3}$$

$$= \frac{54}{3}$$

$$= 18$$

10. B: Since rate in mph $= \frac{\text{distance in miles}}{\text{time in hours}}$, Zeke's driving speed on the way to Atlanta and home from Atlanta in mph can be expressed as $\frac{d}{3}$ and $\frac{d}{2}$, respectively, when $d =$ distance between Zeke's house and his destination. Since Zeke drove 20 mph faster on his way home, $\frac{d}{2} - \frac{d}{3} = 20$.

$$6\left(\frac{d}{2} - \frac{d}{3} = 20\right)$$
$$3d - 2d = 120$$
$$d = 120$$

Since the distance between Zeke's house and the store in Atlanta is 120 miles, Zeke drove a total distance of 240 miles in five hours. Therefore, his average speed was $\frac{240 \text{ miles}}{5 \text{ hours}} = 48$ mph.

11. C: Aaron ran four miles from home and then back again, so he ran a total of eight miles. Therefore, statement III is false. Statements I and II, however, are both true. Since Aaron ran eight miles in eighty minutes, he ran an average of one mile every ten minutes, or six miles per hour; he ran two miles from point A to B in 20 minutes and four miles from D to E in 40 minutes, so his running speed between both sets of points was the same.

12. D: First, use the table to determine the values of $(a * b)$ and $(c * d)$:

*	a	b	c	d
a	d	a	b	c
b	a	b	c	d
c	b	c	d	a
d	c	d	a	b

Since $(a * b) = a$ and $(c * d) = a$, that means $(a * b) * (c * d) = a * a$, which is equal to d.

13. B: When $y = x^3$, $x = \sqrt[3]{y}$. Similarly, when $y = e^x$, $x = \ln y$ for $y > 0$. On the other hand, when $y = x + a$, $x = y - a$; when $y = \frac{1}{x}$, $x = \frac{1}{y}$ for $x, y \neq 0$; and when $y = \sin x$, $x = \sin^{-1} y$.

14. B: Deductive reasoning moves from one or more general statements to a specific, while inductive reasoning makes a general conclusion based on a series of specific instances or observations. Whenever the premises used in deductive reasoning are true, the conclusion drawn is necessarily true. In inductive reasoning, it is possible for the premises to be true and the conclusion to be false since there may exist an exception to the general conclusion drawn from the observations made.

15. A: The first argument's reasoning is valid, and since its premises are true, the argument is also sound. The second argument's reasoning is invalid; that the premises are true is irrelevant. (For example, consider the true premises "all cats are mammals" and "all dogs are mammals;" it cannot be logically concluded that all dogs are cats.) The third argument's reasoning is valid, but since one of its premises is false, the argument is not sound.

16. C: The logical representation $p \rightarrow q$ means that p implies q. In other words, if p, then q. Unlike the contrapositive (Choice C), neither the converse (choice A) nor the inverse (choice B) is necessarily true. For example, consider this statement: all cats are mammals. This can be written as an if/then statement: if an animal is a cat, then the animal is a mammal. The converse would read, "If an animal is a mammal, then the animal is a cat;" of course, this is not necessarily true since there are many mammals other than cats. The inverse statement, "If an animal is not a cat, then the animal is not a mammal," is false. The contrapositive, "If an animal is not a mammal, then the animal is not a cat" is true since there are no cats which are not mammals.

17. D: The symbol $\wedge$ is the logical conjunction symbol. In order for statement $(p \wedge q)$ to be true, both statements p and q must be true. The $\neg$ symbol means "not," so if $(p \wedge q)$ is true, then $\neg(p \wedge q)$ is false, and if $(p \wedge q)$ is false, then $\neg(p \wedge q)$ is true. The statement $q \leftrightarrow \neg(p \wedge q)$ is true when the value of q is the same as the value of $\neg(p \wedge q)$.

p	q	$(p \wedge q)$	$\neg(p \wedge q)$	$q \leftrightarrow \neg(p \wedge q)$
T	T	T	F	F
T	F	F	T	F
F	T	F	T	T
F	F	F	T	F

18. D: The value "0" means "false," and the value "1" means "true." For the logical disjunction "or," the output value is true if either or both input values are true, else it is false. For the logical conjunction "and," the output value is true only if both input values are true. "Not A" is true when A is false and is false when A is true.

X	Y	Z	not Y	not Z	not Y or not Z	X and (not Y or not Z)
0	0	0	1	1	1	0
0	0	1	1	0	1	0
0	1	0	0	1	1	0
0	1	1	0	0	0	0
1	0	0	1	1	1	1
1	0	1	1	0	1	1
1	1	0	0	1	1	1
1	1	1	0	0	0	0

19. A: The Babylonians used a base-60 numeral system, which is still used in the division of an hour into 60 minutes, a minute into 60 seconds, and a circle into 360 degrees. The word "algebra" and its development as a discipline separate from geometry are attributed to the Arabic/Islamic civilization. The Greek philosopher Thales is credited with using deductive reasoning to prove geometric concepts. Boolean logic was introduced by British mathematician George Boole.

20. C: Leonhard Euler made many important contributions to the field of mathematics. One such contribution, Euler's formula $e^{i\varphi} = \cos\varphi + i\sin\varphi = 0$, can be written as $e^{i\pi} + 1 = 0$ when $\varphi = \pi$.

21. B: The notation $\mathbb{P} \subseteq \mathbb{N} \subseteq \mathbb{Z} \subseteq \mathbb{Q} \subseteq \mathbb{R} \subseteq \mathbb{C}$ means that the set of prime numbers is a subset of the set natural numbers, which is a subset of the set of integers, which is a subset of the set of rational numbers, which is a subset of the set real numbers, which is a subset of the set of complex numbers.

22. A: The set of whole numbers, $\{0, 1, 2, 3, \dots\}$, does not contain the number -4. Since -4 is an integer, it is also a rational number and a real number.

23. D: In order for a set to be a group under an operation, it must be closed and demonstrate associativity under the operation, there must exist an identity element, and for every element in the group, there must exist an inverse element in the group.

The set of prime numbers under multiplication is not closed. For example, $2 \times 3 = 6$, and 6 is not a member of the set of prime numbers. Similarly, the set of negative integers under subtraction is not closed since subtracting two negative integers can yield a positive integer. Though the set of counting numbers under addition is closed, it is not is associative, and there exists no identity element (the number zero in this case) in the group. The set of complex numbers other than zero under multiplication is closed and associative; the identity 1 is a member of the group, and for each element in the group, there is a multiplicative inverse (reciprocal), since zero is excluded.

24. A: First, multiply the numerator and denominator by the denominator's conjugate, $4 + 2i$. Then, simplify the result and write the answer in the form $a + bi$.

$$\frac{2 + 3i}{4 - 2i} \times \frac{4 + 2i}{4 + 2i} = \frac{8 + 4i + 12i + 6i^2}{16 - 4i^2}$$
$$= \frac{8 + 16i - 6}{16 + 4}$$
$$= \frac{2 + 16i}{20}$$
$$= \frac{1}{10} + \frac{4}{5}i$$

25. D: First, simplify the expression within the absolute value symbol.

$$|(2 - 3i)^2 - (1 - 4i)| = |4 - 12i + 9i^2 - 1 + 4i|$$
$$= |4 - 12i - 9 - 1 + 4i|$$
$$= |-6 - 8i|$$

The absolute value of a complex number is its distance from 0 on the complex plane. Use the Pythagorean theorem to find the distance of $-6 - 8i$ from the origin. Since the distance from the origin to the point $-6 - 8i$ is 10, $|-6 - 8i| = 10$.

26. B: In order for a set to be a group under operation $*$:

- The set must be closed under that operation. In other words, when the operation is performed on any two members of the set, the result must also be a member of that set.
- The set must demonstrate associativity under the operation: $a * (b * c) = (a * b) * c$
- There must exist an identity element e in the group: $a * e = e * a = a$
- For every element in the group, there must exist an inverse element in the group: $a * b = b * a = e$

Choice A can easily be eliminated as the correct answer because the set $\{-i, 0, i\}$ does not contain the multiplicative identity 1. Though choices C and D contain the element 1, neither is closed: for example, since $i \times i = -1$, -1 must be an element of the group. Choice B is closed, contains the multiplicative identity 1, and the inverse of each element is included in the set as well. Of course, multiplication is an associative operation, so the set $\{-1, 1, i, -i\}$ forms a group under multiplication

$\times$	-1	1	i	$-i$
-1	1	-1	$-i$	i
1	-1	1	i	$-i$
i	$-i$	i	-1	1
$-i$	i	$-i$	1	-1

27. D: The identity element is d since $d\#a = a\#d = a, d\#b = b\#d = b, d\#c = c\#d = c$, and $d\#d = d$. The inverse of element c is c since $c\#c = d$, the identity element. The operation # is commutative because $a\#b = b\#a, a\#c = c\#a$, etc. Rather than check that the operation is commutative for each pair of elements, note that elements in the table display symmetry about the diagonal elements; this indicates that the operation is indeed commutative.

#	a	b	c	d
a	c	d	b	a
b	d	c	a	b
c	b	a	d	c
d	a	b	c	d

28. C: "The square of twice the sum of x and three is equal to the product of twenty-four and x" is represented by the equation $[2(x + 3)]^2 = 24x$. Solve for x.

$$[2x + 6]^2 = 24x$$
$$4x^2 + 24x + 36 = 24x$$
$$4x^2 = -36$$
$$x^2 = -9$$
$$x = \pm\sqrt{-9}$$
$$x = \pm 3i$$

So, $-3i$ is a possible value of x.

29. C: If x is a prime number and the greatest common factor of x and y is greater than 1, the greatest common factor of x and y must be x. The least common multiple of two numbers is equal to the product of those numbers divided by their greatest common factor. So, the least common multiple of x and y is $\frac{xy}{x} = y$. Therefore, the values in the two columns are the same.

30. D: Since a and b are even integers, each can be expressed as the product of 2 and an integer. So, if we write $a = 2x$ and $b = 2y$, $3(2x)^2 + 9(2y)^3 = c$.

$$3(4x^2) + 9(8y^3) = c$$
$$12x^2 + 72y^3 = c$$
$$12(x^2 + 6y^3) = c$$

Since c is the product of 12 and some other integer, 12 must be a factor of c. Incidentally, the numbers 2, 3, and 6 must also be factors of c since each is also a factor of 12.

31. C: Choice C is the equation for the greatest integer function. A function is a relationship in which for every element of the domain (x), there is exactly one element of the range (y). Graphically, a relationship between x and y can be identified as a function if the graph passes the vertical line test.

The first relation is a parabola on its side, which fails the vertical line test for functions. A circle (Choice B) also fails the vertical line test and is therefore not a function. The relation in Choice D pairs two elements of the range with one of the elements of the domain, so it is also not a function.

32. B: The area of a triangle is $A = \frac{1}{2}bh$, where b and h are the lengths of the triangle's base and height, respectively. The base of the given triangle is x, but the height is not given. Since the triangle is a right triangle and the hypotenuse is given, the triangle's height can be found using the Pythagorean theorem.

$$x^2 + h^2 = 6^2$$
$$h = \sqrt{36 - x^2}$$

To find the area of the triangle in terms of x, substitute $\sqrt{36 - x^2}$ for the height and x for the base of the triangle into the area formula, $\left(A = \frac{1}{2}bh\right)$:

$$A(x) = \frac{1}{2}(x)(\sqrt{36 - x^2})$$

$$A(x) = \frac{x\sqrt{36 - x^2}}{2}$$

33. A: Substitute and simplify:

$$\begin{aligned}
[g \circ f\,]x &= g(f(x)) \\
&= g(2x + 4) \\
&= (2x + 4)^2 - 3(2x + 4) + 2 \\
&= 4x^2 + 16x + 16 - 6x - 12 + 2 \\
&= 4x^2 + 10x + 6
\end{aligned}$$

34. C: One way to approach the problem is to use the table of values to first write equations for $f(x)$ and $g(x)$: $f(x) = 2x^2$ and $g(x) = 2x + 5$. Then, use those equations to find $f(g(-4))$.

$$g(-4) = 2(-4) + 5 = -3$$
$$f(-3) = 2(-3)^2 = 18$$

So, $f(g(-4)) = 18$.

35. D: By definition, when $f(x)$ and $g(x)$ are inverse functions, $f(g(x)) = g(f(x)) = x$. So, $f(g(4)) = 4$.

36. B: To find the inverse of an equation, solve for x in terms of y; then, exchange the variables x and y. Or, to determine if two functions $f(x)$ and $g(x)$ are inverses, find $f(g(x))$ and $g(f(x))$; if both results are x, then $f(x)$ and $g(x)$ are inverse functions.

For example, to find the inverse of $y = x + 6$, rewrite the equation $x = y + 6$ and solve for y. Since $y = x - 6$, the two given equations given in Choice A are inverses. Likewise, to find the inverse of $y = \frac{2x+3}{x-1}$, rewrite the equation as $x = \frac{2y+3}{y-1}$ and solve for y:

$$\begin{aligned}
xy - x &= 2y + 3 \\
xy - 2y &= x + 3 \\
y(x - 2) &= x + 3 \\
y &= \frac{x + 3}{x - 2}
\end{aligned}$$

The two equations given in Choice C are inverses.

Choice B: $y = 2(2x + 3) - 3 = 4x + 6$. The two given equations are **NOT** inverses.

Choice D: $y = \frac{(2x+1)-1}{2} = \frac{2x}{2} = x$ and $y = 2\left(\frac{x-1}{2}\right) + 1 = x - 1 + 1 = x$, so the two given equations are inverses.

37. A: Below is the graph of $g(x)$.

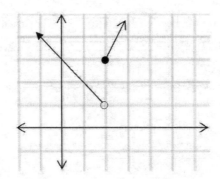

Statement II is true: the graph is indeed discontinuous at $x = 2$. Since $g(3) = 2(3) - 1 = 5$, Statement I is false, and since the range is $y > 1$, Statement III is also false.

38. A: In the range $(-\infty, -1)$, the graph represented is $y = x^2$. In the range $[-1,2)$, the graph is the greatest integer function, $y = [\![x]\!]$. In the range $[2, \infty)$, the graph is $y = -2x + 6$.

39. B: If $y = a(x + b)(x + c)^2$, the degree of the polynomial is 3. Since the degree of the polynomial is odd and the leading coefficient is positive $(a > 0)$, the end behavior of the graph goes to (∞, ∞) and $(-\infty, -\infty)$. Therefore, neither Choice A nor Choice C can be a graph of $y = a(x + b)(x + c)^2$. The maximum number of critical points in the graph is at most one less than the degree of the polynomial, so Choice D, cannot be the graph of the function. Choice B displays the correct end behavior and has two bumps, so it is a possible graph of $y = a(x + b)(x + c)^2$.

40. B: $5n + 3s \geq 300$ where n is the number of non-student tickets which must be sold and s is the number of student tickets which must be sold. The intercepts of this linear inequality are $n = 60$ and $s = 100$. The solid line through the two intercepts represents the minimum number of each type of ticket which must be sold in order to offset production costs. All points above the line represent sales which result in a profit for the school.

41. D: The vertex form of a quadratic equation is $y = a(x - h)^2 + k$, where $x = h$ is the parabola's axis of symmetry and (h, k) is the parabola's vertex. The vertex of the graph is $(-1,3)$, so the equation can be written as $y = a(x + 1)^2 + 3$. The parabola passes through point $(1,1)$, so $1 = a(1 + 1)^2 + 3$. Solve for a:

$$1 = a(1 + 1)^2 + 3$$
$$1 = a(2)^2 + 3$$
$$1 = 4a + 3$$
$$-2 = 4a$$
$$-\frac{1}{2} = a$$

So, the vertex form of the parabola is $y = -\frac{1}{2}(x+1)^2 + 3$. Write the equation in the form $y = ax^2 + bx + c$.

$$y = -\frac{1}{2}(x+1)^2 + 3$$

$$y = -\frac{1}{2}(x^2 + 2x + 1) + 3$$

$$y = -\frac{1}{2}x^2 - x - \frac{1}{2} + 3$$

$$y = -\frac{1}{2}x^2 - x + \frac{5}{2}$$

42. D: There are many ways to solve quadratic equations in the form $ax^2 + bx + c = 0$; however, some methods, such as graphing and factoring, may not be useful for some equations, such as those with irrational or complex roots. Solve this equation by completing the square or by using the Quadratic Formula, $x = \frac{-b \pm \sqrt{b^2 - 4ac}}{2a}$. Given $7x^2 + 6x + 2 = 0$; $a = 7, b = 6, c = 2$:

$$x = \frac{-6 \pm \sqrt{6^2 - 4(7)(2)}}{2(7)}$$

$$x = \frac{-6 \pm \sqrt{36 - 56}}{14}$$

$$x = \frac{-6 \pm \sqrt{-20}}{14}$$

$$x = \frac{-6 \pm 2i\sqrt{5}}{14}$$

$$x = \frac{-3 \pm i\sqrt{5}}{7}$$

43. C: A system of linear equations can be solved by using matrices or by using the graphing, substitution, or elimination (also called linear combination) method. The elimination method is shown here:

$$3x + 4y = 2$$
$$2x + 6y = -2$$

In order to eliminate x by linear combination, multiply the top equation by 2 and the bottom equation by −3 so that the coefficients of the x-terms will be additive inverses.

$$2(3x + 4y = 2)$$
$$-3(2x + 6y = -2)$$

Then, add the two equations and solve for y.

$$6x + 8y = 4$$
$$\underline{-6x - 18y = 6}$$
$$-10y = 10$$
$$y = -1$$

Substitute -1 for y in either of the given equations and solve for x.

$$3x + 4(-1) = 2$$
$$3x - 4 = 2$$
$$3x = 6$$
$$x = 2$$

The solution to the system of equations is $(2, -1)$.

44. C: The graph below shows that the lines are parallel and that the shaded regions do not overlap. There is no solution to $6x + 2y \leq 12$ and $3x \geq 8 - y$.

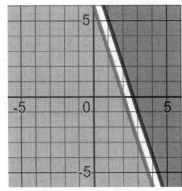

$$6x + 2y \leq 12$$
$$2y \leq -6x + 12$$
$$y \leq -3x + 6$$

$$3x \geq 8 - y$$
$$y \geq -3x + 8$$

45. A: First, write three equations from the information given in the problem. Since the total number of tickets sold was 810, $x + y + z = 810$. The ticket sales generated \$14,500, so $15x + 25y + 20z = 14,500$. The number of children under ten was the same as twice the number of adults and seniors, so $x = 2(y + z)$, which can be rewritten as $x - 2y - 2z = 0$.

The coefficients of each equation are arranged in the rows of a 3×3 matrix, which, when multiplied by the 3×1 matrix arranging the variables $x, y,$ and z, will give the 3×1 matrix which arranges the constants of the equations.

46. B: Multiply the second equation by 2 and combine it with the first equation to eliminate y.

$$2x\ -4y\ +1z\ =\ 10$$
$$\underline{+\ -6x\ +4y\ -8z\ =\ -14}$$
$$-4x\qquad -7z\ =\ -4$$

Multiply the third equation by –2 and combine it with the original second equation to eliminate y.

$$-3x\ +2y\ -4z\ =\ -7$$
$$\underline{+\ -2x\ -2y\ +6z\ =\ 2}$$
$$-5x\qquad +2z\ =\ -5$$

124

Multiply the equation from step one by 5 and the equation from step two by -4 and combine to eliminate x.

$$
\begin{array}{rcr}
-20x -35z &=& -20 \\
+\quad 20x - 8z &=& 20 \\
\hline
-43z &=& 0 \\
z &=& 0
\end{array}
$$

Substitute 0 for z in the equation from step 2 to find x.

$$
\begin{aligned}
-5x + 2(0) &= -5 \\
-5x &= -5 \\
x &= 1
\end{aligned}
$$

Substitute 0 for z and 1 for x into the first original equation to find y.

$$
\begin{aligned}
2(1) - 4y + (0) &= 10 \\
2 - 4y &= 10 \\
-4y &= 8 \\
y &= -2
\end{aligned}
$$

47. B: One way to solve the equation is to write $x^4 + 64 = 20x^2$ in the quadratic form:

$$(x^2)^2 - 20(x^2) + 64 = 0$$

This trinomial can be factored as $(x^2 - 4)(x^2 - 16) = 0$. In each set of parentheses is a difference of squares, which can be factored further: $(x + 2)(x - 2)(x + 4)(x - 4) = 0$. Use the zero product property to find the solutions to the equation.

$$
\begin{array}{llll}
x + 2 = 0 & x - 2 = 0 & x + 4 = 0 & x - 4 = 0 \\
\quad x = -2 & \quad x = 2 & \quad x = -4 & \quad x = 4
\end{array}
$$

48. A: First, set the equation equal to zero, then factor it.

$$
\begin{aligned}
3x^3y^2 - 45x^2y &= 15x^3y - 9x^2y^2 \\
3x^3y^2 - 15x^3y + 9x^2y^2 - 45x^2y &= 0 \\
3x^2y(xy - 5x + 3y - 15) &= 0 \\
3x^2y[x(y - 5) + 3(y - 5)] &= 0 \\
3x^2y[(y - 5)(x + 3)] &= 0
\end{aligned}
$$

Use the zero product property to find the solutions.

$$
\begin{array}{lll}
3x^2y = 0 & y - 5 = 0 & x + 3 = 0 \\
\quad x = 0 & \quad y = 5 & \quad x = -3 \\
\quad y = 0 & &
\end{array}
$$

So, the solutions are $x = \{0, -3\}$ and $y = \{0,5\}$.

49. D: The degree of $f(x)$ is 1, the degree of $g(x)$ is 2, and the degree of $h(x)$ is 3. The leading coefficient for each function is 2. Functions $f(x)$ and $h(x)$ have exactly one real zero ($x = 1$), while $g(x)$ has two real zeros ($x = \pm 1$):

$$
\begin{array}{ccc}
f(x) = 0 & g(x) = 0 & h(x) = 0 \\
2x - 2 = 0 & 2x^2 - 2 = 0 & 2x^3 - 2 = 0 \\
2x = 2 & 2x^2 = 2 & 2x^3 = 2 \\
x = 1 & x^2 = 1 & x^3 = 1 \\
& x = 1; x = -1 & x = 1
\end{array}
$$

50. B: The path of a bullet is a parabola, which is the graph of a quadratic function. The path of a sound wave can be modeled by a sine or cosine function. The distance an object travels over time given a constant rate is a linear relationship, while radioactive decay is modeled by an exponential function.

51. B: First, use the properties of logarithms to solve for y:

$$
\begin{aligned}
2\log_4 y + \log_4 16 &= 3 \\
\log_4 y^2 + \log_4 16 &= 3 \\
\log_4 16\,y^2 &= 3 \\
16y^2 &= 4^3 \\
16y^2 &= 64 \\
y^2 &= 4 \\
y &= 2
\end{aligned}
$$

Finally, substitute 2 for y in the expression $\log_y 256$ and simplify: $\log_2 256 = 8$ since $2^8 = 256$.

52. B: First, apply the laws of exponents to simplify the expression on the left. Then, add the two fractions:

$$
\begin{aligned}
\frac{(x^2y)(2xy^{-2})^3}{16x^5y^2} + \frac{3}{xy} &= \frac{(x^2y)(8x^3y^{-6})}{16x^5y^2} + \frac{3}{xy} \\
&= \frac{8x^5y^{-5}}{16x^5y^2} + \frac{3}{xy} \\
&= \frac{1}{2y^7} + \frac{3}{xy} \\
&= \frac{1}{2y^7} \times \frac{x}{x} + \frac{3}{xy} \times \frac{2y^6}{2y^6} \\
&= \frac{x}{2xy^7} + \frac{6y^6}{2xy^7} \\
&= \frac{x + 6y^6}{2xy^7}
\end{aligned}
$$

53. C: If $f(x) = 10^x$ and $f(x) = 5$, then $5 = 10^x$. Since $\log_{10} x$ is the inverse of 10^x, $\log_{10} 5 = \log_{10}(10^x) = x$. Therefore, $0.7 \approx x$.

54. C: The x-intercept is the point at which $f(x) = 0$. When $0 = \log_b x$, $b^0 = x$; since $b^0 = 1$, the x-intercept of $f(x) = \log_b x$ is always 1. If $f(x) = \log_b x$ and $x = b$, then $f(x) = \log_b b$, which is, by definition, 1. ($b^1 = b$). If $g(x) = b^x$, then $f(x)$ and $g(x)$ are inverse functions and are therefore symmetric with respect to $y = x$. The statement choice C is not necessarily true since $x < 1$ includes numbers less than or equal to zero, the values for which the function is undefined. The statement $f(x) < 0$ is true only for x values between 0 and 1 ($0 < x < 1$).

55. C: The graph shown is the exponential function $y = 2^x$. Notice that the graph passes through $(-2, 0.25)$, $(0,1)$, and $(2,4)$. A quick check of each option demonstrates the fit:

x	x^2	$\sqrt{x}$	2^x	$\log_2 x$
-2	4	undefined in $\mathbb{R}$	0.25	undefined
0	0	0	1	undefined
2	4	$\sqrt{2}$	4	1

56. D: Bacterial growth is exponential. Let x be the number of doubling times and a be the number of bacteria in the colony originally transferred into the broth and y be the number of bacteria in the broth after a doubling times. After 1 hour the population would have doubled three times:

$$a(2^3) = 8 \times 10^6$$
$$8a = 8 \times 10^6$$
$$a = 10^6$$

The equation for determining the number of bacteria is $y = (2^x) \times 10^6$. Since the bacteria double every twenty minutes, they go through three doubling times every hour. So, when the bacteria are allowed to grow for eight hours, they will have gone through 24 doubling times. When $x = 24$, $y = (2^{24}) \times 10^6 = 16,777,216 \times 10^6$, which is approximately 1.7×10^{13}.

57. B: Since the pH scale is a base–10 logarithmic scale, a difference in pH of 1 indicates a ratio between strengths of 10. So, an acid with a pH of 3 is 10 times stronger than an acid with a pH of 4.

58. A: Get as many terms as possible out from the radical and any radicals out from the denominator:

$$\sqrt{\frac{-28x^6}{27y^5}} = \sqrt{\frac{-4x^6 \times (7)}{9y^4 \times (3y)}}$$

$$= \sqrt{\frac{-(2x^3)^2 \times (7)}{(3y^2)^2 \times (3y)}}$$

$$= \frac{2x^3 i\sqrt{7}}{3y^2\sqrt{3y}} \times \frac{\sqrt{3y}}{\sqrt{3y}}$$

$$= \frac{2x^3 i\sqrt{21y}}{9y^3}$$

59. C: Evaluate each option following the order of operations and using the properties of inequalities:

$$-4 \leq 2 + 3(x-1) \leq 2$$
$$-6 \leq 3(x-1) \leq 0$$
$$-2 \leq x - 1 \leq 0$$
$$-1 \leq x \leq 1$$

$$-2x^2 + 2 \geq x^2 - 1$$
$$-3x^2 \geq -3$$
$$x^2 \leq 1$$
$$-1 \leq x \leq 1$$

$$\frac{11 - |3x|}{7} \geq 2$$
$$11 - |3x| \geq 14$$
$$-|3x| \geq 3$$
$$|3x| \leq -3$$
$$\text{No solution}$$

$$3|2x| + 4 \leq 10$$
$$3|2x| \leq 6$$
$$|2x| \leq 2$$
$$-2 \leq 2x \leq 2$$
$$-1 \leq x \leq 1$$

60. D: When solving radical equations, check for extraneous solutions.

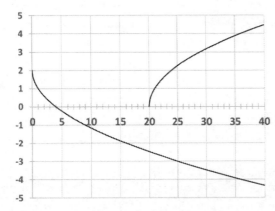

$$2 - \sqrt{x} = \sqrt{x - 20}$$
$$\left(2 - \sqrt{x}\right)^2 = \left(\sqrt{x - 20}\right)^2$$
$$4 - 4\sqrt{x} + x = x - 20$$
$$-4\sqrt{x} = -24$$
$$\sqrt{x} = 6$$
$$x = 36$$

$$2 - \sqrt{36} = \sqrt{36 - 20}$$
$$2 - 6 = \sqrt{16}$$
$$-4 \neq 4$$

Since the solution does not check, there is no solution. Notice that the graphs $y = 2 - \sqrt{x}$ and $y = \sqrt{x - 20}$ do not intersect, which confirms there is no solution.

61. B: Notice that choice C cannot be correct since $x \neq 1$. ($x = 1$ results in a zero in the denominator.)

$$\frac{x-2}{x-1} = \frac{x-1}{x+1} + \frac{2}{x-1}$$
$$\frac{x-4}{x-1} = \frac{x-1}{x+1}$$
$$(x+1)(x-4) = (x-1)(x-1)$$
$$x^2 - 3x - 4 = x^2 - 2x + 1$$
$$-5 = x$$

62. A: A simple test of each option at $x = -2, 0$, and 1 demonstrates that only option A works:

x	Observed	y_a	y_b	y_c
-2	~1	$\frac{3}{4}$	$-\frac{3}{4}$	$-\frac{5}{4}$
0	$-\frac{3}{2}$	$-\frac{3}{2}$	$-\frac{3}{2}$	$\frac{1}{2}$
1	$-\frac{3}{2}$	$-\frac{3}{2}$	-3	$-\frac{1}{2}$

63. A: An easy way to determine which is the graph of $f(x) = -2|-x + 4| - 1$ is to find $f(x)$ for a few values of x. For example, $f(0) = -2|0 + 4| - 1 = -9$. Graphs A and B pass through $(0, -9)$, but graphs C and D do not. $f(4) = -2|-4 + 4| - 1 = -1$. Graphs A and D pass through $(4, -1)$, but graphs B and C do not. Graph A is the correct graph.

64. C: The first function shifts the graph of $y = \frac{1}{x}$ to the right one unit and up one unit. The domain and range of $y = \frac{1}{x}$ are $\{x: x \neq 0\}$ and $\{y: y \neq 0\}$, so the domain and range of $y = \frac{1}{x-1} + 1$ are $\{x: x \neq 1\}$ and $\{y: y \neq 1\}$. The element 1 is not in its domain.

The second function inverts the graph of $y = \sqrt{x}$ and shifts it to the left two units and down one unit. The domain and range of $y = \sqrt{x}$ are $\{x: x \geq 0\}$ and $\{y: y \geq 0\}$, so the domain and range of $y = -\sqrt{x+2} - 1$ are $\{x: x \geq -2\}$ and $\{y: y \leq -1\}$. The range does not contain the element 2.

The third function shifts the graph of $y = |x|$ to the left two units and down three units. The domain of $y = |x|$ is the set of all real numbers and range is $\{y: y \geq 0\}$, so the domain of $y = |x + 2| - 3$ is the set of all real numbers and the range is $\{y: y \geq -3\}$. The domain contains the element 1 and the range contains the element 2.

This is the graph of the fourth function. The domain of this piece-wise function is the set of all real numbers, and the range is $\{y: y < -1\}$. The range does not contain the element 2.

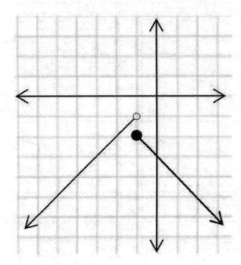

65. B: First, state the exclusions of the domain.

$$x^3 + 2x^2 - x - 2 \neq 0$$
$$(x + 2)(x - 1)(x + 1) \neq 0$$
$$x + 2 \neq 0 \quad x - 1 \neq 0 \quad x + 1 \neq 0$$
$$x \neq -2 \qquad x \neq 1 \qquad x \neq -1$$

To determine whether there are asymptotes or holes at these values of x, simplify the expression:

$$\frac{x^2 - x - 6}{x^3 + 2x^2 - x - 2} = \frac{(x - 3)(x + 2)}{(x + 2)(x - 1)(x + 1)} = \frac{x - 3}{(x - 1)(x + 1)}$$

There are asymptotes at $x = 1$ and at $x = -1$ and a hole at $x = -2$. Statement I is false.

To find the x-intercept of $f(x)$, solve $f(x) = 0$. $f(x) = 0$ when the numerator is equal to zero. The numerator equals zero when $x = -2$ and $x = 3$; however, -2 is excluded from the domain of $f(x)$, so the x-intercept is 3. To find the y-intercept of $f(x)$, find $f(0)$.

$$\frac{0^2 - 0 - 6}{0^3 + 2(0)^2 - 0 - 2} = \frac{-6}{-2} = 3$$

The y-intercept is 3. Statement II is true.

66. C: Start by setting up a proportion to solve by cross multiplication: $\frac{1 \text{ inch}}{60 \text{ feet}} = \frac{10 \text{ inches}}{x \text{ feet}}$. When the numbers are cross multiplied, you get $x = 600$ feet. Now we need to convert 600 feet to yards. There are 3 feet in 1 yard, so divide 600 by 3 to find the number of yards between the two points: $600 \div 3 = 200$ yards.

67. C: The period of the pendulum is a function of the square root of the length of its string, and is independent of the mass of the pendulum or the angle from which it is released. If the period of Pendulum 1's swing is four times the period of Pendulum 2's swing, then the length of Pendulum 1's string must be 16 times the length of Pendulum 2's swing since all other values besides L in the expression $2\pi\sqrt{\dfrac{L}{g}}$ remain the same.

68. D: There are many ways Josephine may have applied her knowledge to determine how to approximately measure her medicine using her plastic spoon. The only choice which correctly uses dimensional analysis is choice D: the dosage

$$\approx 25 \text{ cc} \times \frac{1 \text{ ml}}{1 \text{ cc}} \times \frac{1\text{L}}{1,000\text{ml}} \times \frac{0.5 \text{ gal}}{2\text{L}} \times \frac{16\text{c}}{1 \text{ gal}} \times \frac{48\text{t}}{1\text{c}} \times \frac{1 \text{ spoonful}}{1\text{t}} \approx \frac{25 \times 16 \times 48}{1,000 \times 4} \approx 5$$

69. D: If the distance between the two houses is 10 cm on the map, then the actual distance between the houses is 100 m. To find x, use the Pythagorean theorem:

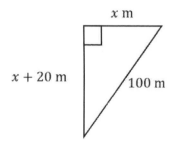

$$x^2 + (x + 20)^2 = (100)^2$$
$$x^2 + x^2 + 40x + 400 = 10,000$$
$$2x^2 + 40x - 9,600 = 0$$
$$2(x^2 + 20x - 4,800) = 0$$
$$2(x - 60)(x + 80) = 0$$
$$x = 60 \quad x = -80$$

Since x represents a distance, it cannot equal –80. Since $x = 60$, $x + 20 = 80$. Roxana walks a total of 140 m to get to her friend's house.

70. D: $\triangle ABC$ is similar to the smaller triangle with which it shares vertex A. $\overline{AB} = (2x - 1) + (x + 7) = 3x + 6$. $AC = 4 + 8 = 12$. Set up a proportion and solve for x:

$$\frac{3x + 6}{12} = \frac{2x - 1}{4}$$
$$12x + 24 = 24x - 12$$
$$36 = 12x$$
$$3 = x$$

So, $\overline{AB} = 3x + 6 = 3(3) + 6 = 15$.

71. B: Percent error $= \dfrac{|\text{actual value}-\text{measured value}|}{\text{actual value}} \times 100\%$, and the average percent error is the sum of the percent errors for each trial divided by the number of trials.

	Percent Error Trial 1	Percent Error Trial 2	Percent Error Trial 3	Percent Error Trial 4	Average Percent Error
Scale 1	0.1%	0.2%	0.2%	0.1%	0.15%
Scale 2	2.06%	2.09%	2.10%	2.08%	2.08%

The percent error for Scale 1 is less than the percent error for Scale 2, so it is more accurate. The more precise scale is Scale 2 because its range of values, 10.210 g − 10.206 g = 0.004 g, is smaller than the Scale 2's range of values, 10.02 g − 9.98 g = 0.04 g.

72. C: If l and w represent the length and width of the enclosed area, its perimeter is equal to $2l + 2w$; since the fence is positioned x feet from the lot's edges on each side, the perimeter of the lot is $2(l + 2x) + 2(w + 2x)$. Since the amount of money saved by fencing the smaller area is $432, and since the fencing material costs $12 per linear foot, 36 fewer feet of material are used to fence around the playground than would have been used to fence around the lot. This can be expressed as the equation:

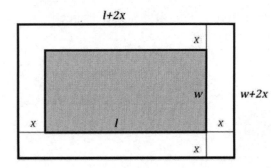

$$2(l + 2x) + 2(w + 2x) - (2l + 2w) = 36$$
$$2l + 4x + 2w + 4x - 2l - 2w = 36$$
$$8x = 36$$
$$x = 4.5 \text{ ft}$$

The difference in the area of the lot and the enclosed space is 141 yd², which is the same as 1,269 ft². So, $(l + 2x)(w + 2x) - lw = 1{,}269$. Substituting 4.5 for x,

$$(l + 9)(w + 9) - lw = 1{,}269$$
$$lw + 9l + 9w + 81 - lw = 1{,}269$$
$$9l + 9w = 1{,}188$$
$$9(l + w) = 1{,}188$$
$$l + w = 132 \text{ ft}$$

Therefore, the perimeter of the enclosed space, $2(l + w)$, is $2(132) = 264$ ft. The cost of 264 ft of fencing is $264 \times \$12 = \$3{,}168$.

73. B: The volume of Natasha's tent is $\frac{x^2 h}{3}$. If she were to increase by 1 ft the length of each side of the square base, the tent's volume would be $\frac{(x+1)^2 h}{3} = \frac{(x^2+2x+1)(h)}{3} = \frac{x^2 h + 2xh + h}{3} = \frac{x^2 h}{3} + \frac{2xh + h}{3}$. Notice this is the volume of Natasha's tent, $\frac{x^2 h}{3}$, increased by $\frac{2xh + h}{3}$, or $\frac{h(2x+1)}{3}$.

132

74. A: The area of a circle is πr^2, so the area of a semicircle is $\frac{\pi r^2}{2}$. Illustrated below is a method which can be used to find the area of the shaded region.

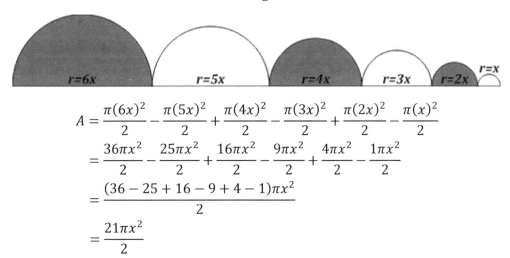

$$A = \frac{\pi(6x)^2}{2} - \frac{\pi(5x)^2}{2} + \frac{\pi(4x)^2}{2} - \frac{\pi(3x)^2}{2} + \frac{\pi(2x)^2}{2} - \frac{\pi(x)^2}{2}$$

$$= \frac{36\pi x^2}{2} - \frac{25\pi x^2}{2} + \frac{16\pi x^2}{2} - \frac{9\pi x^2}{2} + \frac{4\pi x^2}{2} - \frac{1\pi x^2}{2}$$

$$= \frac{(36 - 25 + 16 - 9 + 4 - 1)\pi x^2}{2}$$

$$= \frac{21\pi x^2}{2}$$

75. B: Euclidean geometry is based on the flat plane. One of Euclid's five axioms, from which all Euclidean geometric theorems are derived, is the parallel postulate, which states that in a plane, for any line l and point A not on l, exactly one line which passes through A does not intersect l.

Non-Euclidean geometry considers lines on surfaces that are not flat. For instance, on the Earth's surface, if point A represents the North Pole and line l represents the equator (which does not pass through A), all lines of longitude pass through point A and intersect line l. In elliptical geometry, there are infinitely many lines which pass though A and intersect l, and there is no line which passes through A which does not also intersect l. In hyperbolic geometry when A is not on l, many lines which pass through A diverge from l, or put more succinctly, at least two lines that go through A do not intersect l.

76. C: Sketch a diagram (this one is not to scale) and label the known segments. Use the property that two segments are congruent when they originate from the same point outside of a circle and are tangent to the circle. The point of tangency of $\overline{BC}$ divides the segment into two pieces measuring 4 and 6; the point of tangency of $\overline{AB}$ divides the segment into two pieces measuring 6 and 8; the point of tangency of $\overline{AD}$ divides the segment into two pieces measuring 8 and 4. Therefore $\overline{AD} = 8 + 4 = 12$.

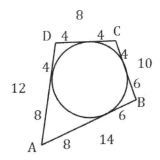

77. B: If the touching edges of the trapezoids are extended, they meet at a point on the horizontal. Using this information and the following geometric relationships, solve for x:

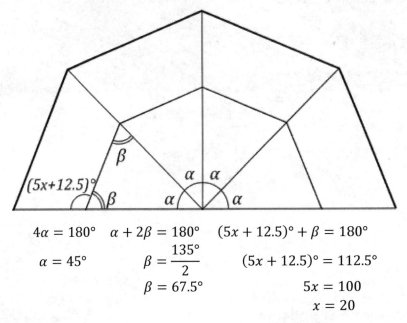

$$4\alpha = 180° \quad \alpha + 2\beta = 180° \quad (5x + 12.5)° + \beta = 180°$$

$$\alpha = 45° \qquad \beta = \frac{135°}{2} \qquad (5x + 12.5)° = 112.5°$$

$$\beta = 67.5° \qquad\qquad 5x = 100$$

$$x = 20$$

78. D: Let b represent the base of the triangle. The height h of the triangle is the altitude drawn from the vertex opposite of b to side b.

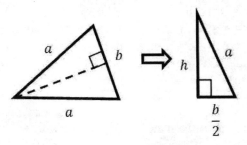

The height of the triangle can be found in terms of a and b by using the Pythagorean theorem:

$$h^2 + \left(\frac{b}{2}\right)^2 = a^2$$

$$h = \sqrt{a^2 - \frac{b^2}{4}}$$

$$= \sqrt{\frac{4a^2 - b^2}{4}}$$

$$= \frac{\sqrt{4a^2 - b^2}}{2}$$

The area of a triangle is $A = \frac{1}{2}bh$, so $A = \frac{1}{2}b\left(\frac{\sqrt{4a^2-b^2}}{2}\right) = \frac{b\sqrt{4a^2-b^2}}{4}$.

79. B: Since $\triangle ADC$ is a right triangle with legs measuring 5 and 12, its hypotenuse measures 13. (5-12-13 is a Pythagorean triple.)

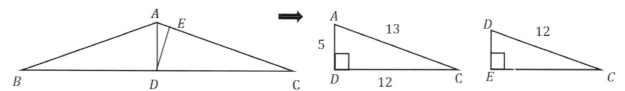

$\triangle ADC$ and $\triangle DEC$ are both right triangles which share vertex C. By the AA similarity theorem $\triangle ADC \sim \triangle DEC$. Therefore, a proportion can be written and solved to find DE.

$$\frac{5}{DE} = \frac{13}{12}$$

$$DE = 4.6$$

80. C: The center of the sphere is shared by the center of the cube, and each of the corners of the cube touches the surface of the sphere. Therefore, the diameter of the sphere is the line which passes through the center of the cube and connects one corner of the cube to the opposite corner on the opposite face. Notice in the illustration below that the diameter d of the sphere can be represented as the hypotenuse of a right triangle with a short leg measuring 4 units. (Since the volume of the cube is 64 cubic units, each of its sides measures $\sqrt[3]{64} = 4$ units.) The long leg of the triangle is the diagonal of the base of the cube. Its length can be found using the Pythagorean theorem: $4^2 + 4^2 = x^2$; $x = \sqrt{32} = 4\sqrt{2}$.

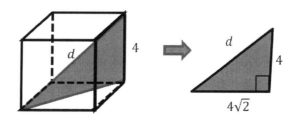

Use the Pythagorean theorem again to find d, the diameter of the sphere: $d^2 = \left(4\sqrt{2}\right)^2 + 4^2$; $d = \sqrt{48} = 4\sqrt{3}$. To find the volume of the sphere, use the formula $V = \frac{4}{3}\pi r^3$. Since the radius r of the sphere is half the diameter, $r = 2\sqrt{3}$, and $V = \frac{4}{3}\pi(2\sqrt{3})^3 = \frac{4}{3}\pi(24\sqrt{3}) = 32\pi\sqrt{3}$ cubic units.

81. D. Since it is given that $\overline{FD} \cong \overline{BC}$ and $\overline{AB} \cong \overline{DE}$, step 2 needs to establish either that $\overline{AC} \cong \overline{EF}$ or that $\triangle ABC \cong \triangle FDE$ in order for step 5 to show that $\triangle ABC \cong \triangle EDF$. The statement $\overline{AC} \cong \overline{EF}$ cannot be shown directly from the given information. On the other hand, $\triangle ABC \cong \triangle FDE$ can be determined: when two parallel lines $\overline{BC} \parallel \overline{FG}$ are cut by a transversal $(\overline{AE})$, alternate exterior angles $(\triangle ABC, \triangle FDE)$ are congruent. Therefore, $\triangle ABC \cong \triangle EDF$ by the side-angle-side (SAS) theorem.

82. A: Step 5 established that $\triangle ABC \cong \triangle EDF$. Because corresponding parts of congruent triangles are congruent (CPCTC), $\angle BAC \cong \angle DEF$. This is useful to establish when trying to prove $\overline{FE} \parallel \overline{AG}$:

when two lines ($\overline{FE}$ and $\overline{AG}$) are cut by a transversal ($\overline{AE}$) and alternate interior angles ($\angle BAC$, $\angle DEF$) are congruent, then the lines are parallel. The completed proof is shown below:

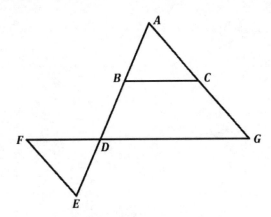

Statement	Reason
1. $\overline{BC} \parallel \overline{FG}$	Given
2. $\angle ABC \cong \angle FDE$	Alternate exterior angles of parallel lines are congruent
3. $\overline{FD} \cong \overline{BC}$	Given
4. $\overline{AB} \cong \overline{DE}$	Given
5. $\triangle ABC \cong \triangle EDF$	SAS
6. $\angle BAC \cong \angle DEF$	CPCTC
7. $\overline{FE} \parallel \overline{AG}$	Alternate interior angles congruent then lines are parallel

Given: $\overline{BC} \parallel \overline{FG}$; $\overline{FD} \cong \overline{BC}$; $\overline{AB} \cong \overline{DE}$
Prove: $\overline{FE} \parallel \overline{AG}$

83. B: A cube has six square faces. The arrangement of these faces in a two-dimensional figure is a net of a cube if the figure can be folded to form a cube. If this is folded, the bottom square in the second column will overlap the fourth square in the top row, so the figure does not represent a net of a cube. The other figures represent three of the eleven possible nets of a cube.

84. D: The cross-section is a hexagon.

85. A: Use the formula for the volume of a sphere to find the radius of the sphere:

$$V = \frac{4}{3}\pi r^3$$
$$36\pi = \frac{4}{3}\pi r^3$$
$$36 = \frac{4}{3}r^3$$
$$27 = r^3$$
$$3 = r$$

Then, substitute the point $(h, k, l) = (1, 0, -2)$ and the radius $r = 3$ into the equation of a sphere:

$$(x - h)^2 + (y - k)^2 + (z - l)^2 = r^2$$
$$(x - 1)^2 + y^2 + (z + 2)^2 = 3^2$$
$$(x - 1)^2 + y^2 + (z + 2)^2 = 9$$
$$x^2 - 2x + 1 + y^2 + z^2 + 4z + 4 = 9$$
$$x^2 + y^2 + z^2 - 2x + 4z = 4$$

86. B: The triangle is a right triangle with legs 3 and 4 units long.

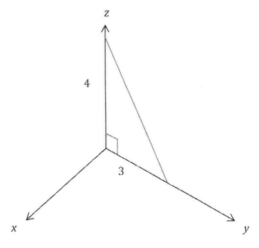

If the triangle is rotated about the z-axis, the solid formed is a cone with a height of 4 and a radius of 3. If the triangle is rotated about the y-axis, the solid formed is a cone with a height of 3 and a radius of 4.

$$V = \frac{1}{3}\pi r^2 h$$
$$V = \frac{1}{3}\pi(3^2)4 \quad V = \frac{1}{3}\pi(4^2)3$$
$$V = 12\pi \qquad V = 16\pi$$

The difference in the volumes of the two cones is $16\pi - 12\pi = 4\pi$ cubic units.

87. D: The point $(5, -5)$ lies on the line segment that has a slope of -2 and passes through $(3, -1)$. If $(5, -5)$ is one of the endpoints of the line segment, then the other would be $(1,3)$.

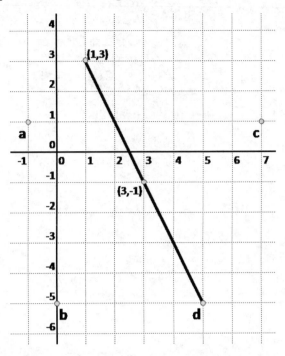

88. D: Since all of the answer choices are parallelograms, determine whether the parallelogram is also a rhombus, a rectangle, or both. One way to do this is by examining the parallelogram's diagonals. If the parallelogram's diagonals are perpendicular, then the parallelogram is a rhombus. If the parallelogram's diagonals are congruent, then the parallelogram is a rectangle. If a parallelogram is both a rhombus and a rectangle, then it is a square. A plot of the quadrilateral would be:

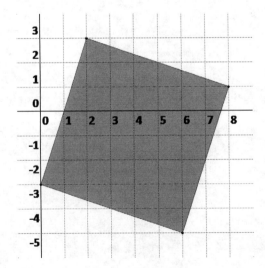

To determine whether the diagonals are perpendicular, find the slopes of the diagonals of the quadrilateral:

Diagonal 1	Diagonal 2
$\dfrac{-5-3}{6-2} = \dfrac{-8}{4} = -2$	$\dfrac{-1-3}{0-8} = \dfrac{-4}{-8} = \dfrac{1}{2}$

The diagonals have opposite inverse slopes and are therefore perpendicular. Thus, the parallelogram is a rhombus. To determine whether the diagonals are congruent, find the lengths of the diagonals of the quadrilateral:

Diagonal 1
$$\sqrt{(6-2)^2 + (-5-3)^2} = \sqrt{(4)^2 + (-8)^2}$$
$$= \sqrt{16+64}$$
$$= \sqrt{80}$$

Diagonal 2
$$\sqrt{(0-8)^2 + (-3-1)^2} = \sqrt{(-8)^2 + (-4)^2}$$
$$= \sqrt{64+16}$$
$$= \sqrt{80}$$

The diagonals are congruent, so the parallelogram is a rectangle. Since the polygon is a rhombus and a rectangle, it is also a square.

89. A: The equation of the circle is given in general form. When the equation is written in the standard form $(x-h)^2 + (y-k)^2 = r^2$, where (h,k) is the center of the circle and r is the radius of the circle, the radius is easy to determine. Putting the equation into standard form requires completing the square for x and y:

$$x^2 - 10x + y^2 + 8y = -29$$
$$(x^2 - 10x + 25) + (y^2 + 8y + 16) = -29 + 25 + 16$$
$$(x-5)^2 + (y+4)^2 = 12$$

Since $r^2 = 12$, and since r must be a positive number, $r = \sqrt{12} = 2\sqrt{3}$.

90. D: One way to determine whether the equation represents an ellipse, a circle, a parabola, or a hyperbola is to find the determinant $b^2 - 4ac$ of the general equation form of a conic section, $ax^2 + bxy + cy^2 + dx + ey + f = 0$, where $a, b, c, d, e,$ and f are constants. Given that the conic section is non-degenerate, if the determinant is positive, then the equation is a hyperbola; if the determinant is negative, then the equation is a circle (when $a = c$ and $b = 0$) or an ellipse; and if the determinant is zero, then the equation is a parabola. For $2x^2 - 3y^2 - 12x + 6y - 15 = 0, a = 2, b = 0, c = -3, d = -12, e = 6,$ and $f = -15$. The determinant $b^2 - 4ac$ is equal to $0^2 - 4(2)(-3) = 24$. Since the determinant is positive, the graph is hyperbolic.

91. B: The graph of $f(x)$ is a parabola with a focus of (a, b) and a directrix of $y = -b$. The axis of symmetry of a parabola passes through the focus and vertex and is perpendicular to the directrix. Since the directrix is a horizontal line, the axis of symmetry is $x = a$; therefore, the x-coordinate of the parabola's vertex must be a. The distance between a point on the parabola and the directrix is equal to the distance between that point and the focus, so the y-coordinate of the vertex must be $y = \dfrac{-b+b}{2} = 0$. So, the vertex of the parabola given by $f(x)$ is $(a, 0)$.

If $g(x)$ were a translation of $f(x)$, as is the case for choices A, C, and D, the vertices of $f(x)$ and $g(x)$ would differ. Since the vertex of the graph of $g(x)$ is $(a, 0)$, none of those choices represent the correct response. However, if $g(x) = -f(x)$, the vertices of the graphs of both functions would be the same; therefore, this represents a possible relation between the two functions.

92. C: When a figure is reflected twice over non-parallel lines, the resulting transformation is a rotation about the point of intersection of the two lines of reflection. The two lines of reflection $y = x + 2$ and $x = 0$ intersect at $(0,2)$. So, $\Delta A''B''C''$ represents a rotation of ΔABC about the point $(0,2)$. The angle of rotation is equal to twice the angle between the two lines of reflection when measured in a clockwise direction from the first to the second line of reflection. Since the angle between the lines or reflection measures $135°$, the angle of rotation which is the composition of the two reflections measures $270°$. All of these properties can be visualized by drawing ΔABC, $\Delta A'B'C'$, and $\Delta A''B''C''$.

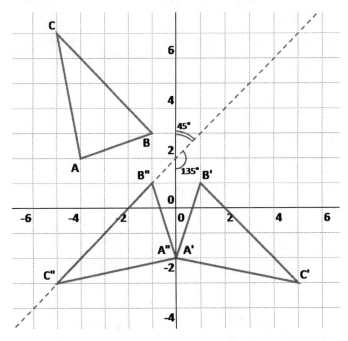

93. B: All regular polygons have rotational symmetry. The angle of rotation is the smallest angle by which the polygon can be rotated such that it maps onto itself; any multiple of this angle will also map the polygon onto itself. The angle of rotation for a regular polygon is the angle formed between two lines drawn from consecutive vertices to the center of the polygon. Since the vertices of a regular polygon lie on a circle, for a regular polygon with n sides, the angle of rotation measures $\frac{360°}{n}$. Therefore, a square has rotational symmetry about the angle $90°$ and its multiples. A regular hexagon has rotational symmetry about the angle $60°$ and its multiples. A regular octagon has rotational symmetry about $45°$ and its multiples. And a regular decagon has rotational symmetry about $36°$ and its multiples. Since $120°$ is a multiple of $60°$, the correct answer is a regular hexagon.

94. A: Since the y-coordinates of points P and Q are the same, line segment $\overline{PQ}$ is a horizontal line segment whose length is the difference in the x-coordinates a and c. Because the length of a line cannot be negative, and because it is unknown whether $a > c$ or $a < c$, $PQ = |a - c|$ or $|c - a|$. Since the x-coordinates of Q and Q' are the same, line segment $\overline{P'Q}$ is a vertical line segment whose length is $|d - b|$ or $|b - d|$. The quadrilateral formed by the transformation of $\overline{PQ}$ to $\overline{P'Q'}$ is a parallelogram. If the base of the parallelogram is $\overline{PQ}$, then the height is $\overline{P'Q}$ since $\overline{PQ} \perp \overline{P'Q}$. For a parallelogram, $A = bh$, so $A = |a - c| \times |b - d|$.

95. B: Determine the veracity of each option given that the hypotenuse of a right triangle is equal to the square root of the sum of the squares of the legs or $c = \sqrt{a^2 + b^2}$:

a. $\tan B = ? \frac{a}{b}$

$\tan B = \dfrac{\text{opposite}}{\text{adjacent}} = \dfrac{b}{a} \neq \dfrac{a}{b}$

b. $\cos B = ? \frac{a\sqrt{a^2+b^2}}{a^2+b^2}$

$\cos B = \dfrac{\text{adjacent}}{\text{hypotenuse}} = \dfrac{a}{\sqrt{a^2+b^2}} = \dfrac{a}{\sqrt{a^2+b^2}} \times \dfrac{\sqrt{a^2+b^2}}{\sqrt{a^2+b^2}} = \dfrac{a\sqrt{a^2+b^2}}{a^2+b^2}$

c. $\sec B = ? \frac{\sqrt{a^2+b^2}}{b}$

$\sec B = \dfrac{\text{hypotenuse}}{\text{adjacent}} = \dfrac{\sqrt{a^2+b^2}}{a} \neq \dfrac{\sqrt{a^2+b^2}}{b}$

d. $\csc B = ? \frac{a^2+b^2}{b}$

$\csc B = \dfrac{\text{hypotenuse}}{\text{opposite}} = \dfrac{\sqrt{a^2+b^2}}{b} \neq \dfrac{a^2+b^2}{b}$

96. C: Find the missing angle measures in the diagram by using angle and triangle properties. Then, use the law of sines to find the distance y between the window and the wife's car: $\dfrac{60}{\sin 15°} = \dfrac{y}{\sin 45°}$, so $y = \dfrac{60 \sin 45°}{\sin 15} \approx 163.9$ ft. Use this number in a sine or cosine function to find x: $\sin 30° \approx \dfrac{x}{163.9}$, so $x \approx 163.9 \sin 30° \approx 82$. Therefore, the man's wife is parked approximately 82 feet from the building.

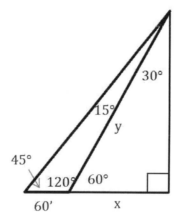

Alternatively, notice that when the man is looking down at a 45-degree angle, the triangle that is formed is an isosceles triangle, meaning that the height of his office is the same as the distance from the office to his car, or $x + 60$ feet. With this knowledge, the problem can be modeled with a single equation:

$$\frac{x+60}{x} = \tan 60° \text{ or } x = \frac{60}{\tan 60°-1}$$

97. A: The reference angle for $-\dfrac{2\pi}{3}$ is $2\pi - \dfrac{2\pi}{3} = \dfrac{4\pi}{3}$, so:

$$\tan\left(-\frac{2\pi}{3}\right) = \tan\left(\frac{4\pi}{3}\right) = \frac{\sin\left(\dfrac{4\pi}{3}\right)}{\cos\left(\dfrac{4\pi}{3}\right)}$$

From the unit circle, the values of $\sin\left(\frac{4\pi}{3}\right)$ and $\cos\left(\frac{4\pi}{3}\right)$ are $-\dfrac{\sqrt{3}}{2}$ and $-\dfrac{1}{2}$, respectively. Therefore:

$$\tan\left(-\frac{2\pi}{3}\right) = \frac{-\dfrac{\sqrt{3}}{2}}{-\dfrac{1}{2}} = \sqrt{3}$$

141

98. D: On the unit circle, $\sin\theta = \frac{1}{2}$ when $\theta = \frac{\pi}{6}$ and when $\theta = \frac{5\pi}{6}$. Since only $\frac{5\pi}{6}$ is in the given range of $\frac{\pi}{2} < \theta < \pi$, $\theta = \frac{5\pi}{6}$.

99. C: Use trigonometric equalities and identities to simplify.

$$\cos\theta\cot\theta = \cos\theta \times \frac{\cos\theta}{\sin\theta} = \frac{\cos^2\theta}{\sin\theta} = \frac{1-\sin^2\theta}{\sin\theta} = \frac{1}{\sin\theta} - \sin\theta = \csc\theta - \sin\theta$$

100. B: The trigonometric identity $\sec^2\theta = \tan^2\theta + 1$ can be used to rewrite the equation $\sec^2\theta = 2\tan\theta$ as $\tan^2\theta + 1 = 2\tan\theta$, which can then be rearranged into the form $\tan^2\theta - 2\tan\theta + 1 = 0$. Solve by factoring and using the zero product property:

$$\tan^2\theta - 2\tan\theta + 1 = 0$$
$$(\tan\theta - 1)^2 = 0$$
$$\tan\theta - 1 = 0$$
$$\tan\theta = 1$$

Since $\tan\theta = 1$ when $\sin\theta = \cos\theta$, for $0 < \theta \le 2\pi$, $\theta = \frac{\pi}{4}$ or $\frac{5\pi}{4}$.

101. A: Since the graph shows a maximum height of 28 inches above the ground, and since the maximum distance from the road the pebble reaches occurs when it is at the top of the tire, the diameter of the tire is 28 inches. Therefore, its radius is 14 inches. From the graph, it can be observed that the tire makes 7.5 rotations in 0.5 seconds. Thus, the tire rotates 15 times in 1 second, or $15 \times 60 = 900$ times per minute.

102. C: The dashed line represents the sine function (x), and the solid line represents a cosine function $g(x)$. The amplitude of $f(x)$ is 4, and the amplitude of $g(x)$ is 2. The function $y = \sin x$ has a period of 2π, while the graph of function $f(x) = a_1\sin(b_1 x)$ has a period of $\frac{6\pi}{1.5} = 4\pi$; therefore, $b_1 = \frac{2\pi}{4\pi} = 0.5$, which is between 0 and 1. The graph of $g(x) = a_2\cos(b_2 x)$ has a period of $\frac{6\pi}{6} = \pi$, so $b_2 = \frac{2\pi}{\pi} = 2$.

103. B: The graph of $f(x)$ is stretched vertically by a factor of 4 with respect to $y = \sin x$, so $a_1 = 4$. The graph of $g(x)$ is stretched vertically by a factor of two and is inverted with respect to the graph of $y = \cos x$, so $a_2 = -2$. Therefore, the statement $a_2 < 0 < a_1$ is true.

104. A: The graph to the right shows the height h in inches of the weight on the spring above the table as a function of time t in seconds. Notice that the height is 3 in above the table at time 0 since the weight was pulled down two inches from its starting position 5 inches above the table. The spring fluctuates 2 inches above and below its equilibrium point, so its maximum height is 7 inches above the table. The graph represents a cosine curve which has been inverted, stretched vertically by a factor of 2, and shifted up five units; also, the graph has been compressed horizontally, with a period of 1 rather than 2π. So, the height of the weight on the spring as a function of time is $h = -2\cos(2\pi t) + 5$.

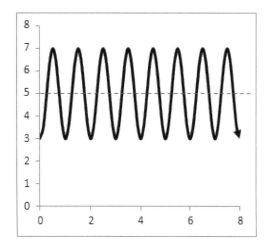

105. C: Since evaluating $\frac{x^3 + 3x^2 - x - 3}{x^2 - 9}$ at $x = -3$ produces a fraction with a zero denominator, simplify the polynomial expression before evaluating the limit:

Simplify the polynomial expression:
$$\frac{x^3 + 3x^2 - x - 3}{x^2 - 9} = \frac{x^2(x+3) - 1(x+3)}{(x+3)(x-3)}$$
$$= \frac{(x+3)(x^2-1)}{(x+3)(x-3)}$$
$$= \frac{(x+1)(x-1)}{x-3}$$

Evaluate the limit:
$$\lim_{x \to -3} \frac{(x+1)(x-1)}{x-3} = \frac{(-3+1)(-3-1)}{-3-3}$$
$$= -\frac{8}{-6}$$
$$= -\frac{4}{3}$$

106. B: To evaluate the limit, divide the numerator and denominator by x^2 and use these properties of limits: $\lim_{x \to \infty} \frac{1}{x} = 0$; the limit of a sum of terms is the sum of the limits of the terms; and the limit of a product of terms is the product of the limits of the terms.

$$\lim_{x \to \infty} \frac{x^2 + 2x - 3}{2x^2 + 1} = \lim_{x \to \infty} \frac{\frac{x^2}{x^2} + \frac{2x}{x^2} - \frac{3}{x^2}}{\frac{2x^2}{x^2} + \frac{1}{x^2}} = \lim_{x \to \infty} \frac{1 + \frac{2}{x} - \frac{3}{x^2}}{2 + \frac{1}{x^2}} = \frac{1 + 0 - 0}{2 + 0} = \frac{1}{2}$$

107. B: Evaluating $\frac{|x-3|}{3-x}$ when $x = 3$ produces a fraction with a zero denominator. To find the limit as x approaches 3 from the right, sketch a graph or make a table of values.

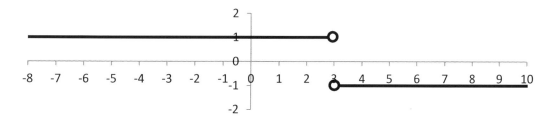

The value of the function approaches –1 as x approaches three from the right, so $\lim_{x \to 3^+} \frac{|x-3|}{3-x} = -1$.

108. C: The slope of the line tangent to the graph of a function f at $x = a$ is $f'(a)$. Since $f(x) = \frac{1}{4}x^2 - 3, f'(x) = 2\left(\frac{1}{4}\right)x^{(2-1)} - 0 = \frac{1}{2}x$. So, the slope at $x = 2$ is $f'(2) = \frac{1}{2}(2) = 1$.

109. D: The definition of the derivative of f at 2, or $f'(2)$, is the limit of the difference quotient $\lim_{h \to 0} \frac{f(2+h)-f(2)}{h}$. Rather than find the limit, simply evaluate the derivative of the function at $x = 2$:

$$f(x) = 2x^3 - 3x^2 + 4$$
$$f'(x) = 6x^2 - 6x$$
$$f'(2) = 6(2)^2 - 6(2)$$
$$f'(2) = 12$$

110. D: To find the derivative, use the Chain Rule $\left(\frac{dy}{dx} = \frac{dy}{du} \times \frac{du}{dx}\right)$:

$$y = e^{3x^2-1}$$

Let $u = 3x^2 - 1 \qquad \rightarrow \qquad \frac{du}{dx} = 6x$

$y = e^u \qquad\qquad\qquad \rightarrow \qquad \frac{dy}{du} = e^u$

$$\frac{dy}{dx} = e^{3x^2-1} \times 6x = 6x\, e^{3x^2-1}$$

111. C: To find the derivative, use the Chain Rule $\left(\frac{dy}{dx} = \frac{dy}{du} \times \frac{du}{dx}\right)$:

$$y = \ln(2x + 1)$$

Let $u = 2x + 1 \qquad \rightarrow \qquad \frac{du}{dx} = 2$

$y = \ln u \qquad\qquad\quad \rightarrow \qquad \frac{dy}{du} = \frac{1}{u}$

$$\frac{dy}{dx} = \left(\frac{1}{2x+1}\right)(2) = \frac{2}{2x+1}$$

112. A: If $\lim_{x \to a^+} f(x) = \lim_{x \to a^-} f(x)$, then $\lim_{x \to a^+} f(x) = \lim_{x \to a^-} f(x) = \lim_{x \to a} f(x)$. Otherwise, $\lim_{x \to a} f(x)$ does not exist. If $\lim_{x \to a} f(x)$ exists, and if $\lim_{x \to a} f(x) = f(a)$, then the function is continuous at a. Otherwise, f is discontinuous at a.

113. A: To find the second derivative of the function, take the derivative of the first derivative of the function:

$$f(x) = 2x^4 - 4x^3 + 2x^2 - x + 1$$
$$f'(x) = 8x^3 - 12x^2 + 4x - 1$$
$$f''(x) = 24x^2 - 24x + 4$$

114. A: The critical points of the graph occur when $f'(x) = 0$.

$$f(x) = 4x^3 - x^2 - 4x + 2$$
$$f'(x) = 12x^2 - 2x - 4$$
$$= 2(6x^2 - x - 2)$$
$$= 2(3x - 2)(2x + 1)$$

$$0 = 2(3x - 2)(2x + 1)$$

$$3x - 2 = 0 \qquad\qquad 2x + 1 = 0$$
$$x = \frac{2}{3} \qquad\qquad\qquad x = -\frac{1}{2}$$

If $f''(x) > 0$ for all x in an interval, the graph of the function is concave upward on that interval, and if $f''(x) < 0$ for all x in an interval, the graph of the function is concave upward on that interval. Find the second derivative of the function and determine the intervals in which $f''(x)$ is less than zero and greater than zero:

$$f''(x) = 24x - 2$$

$$24x - 2 < 0 \qquad\qquad 24x - 2 > 0$$
$$x < \frac{1}{12} \qquad\qquad\qquad x > \frac{1}{12}$$

The graph of f is concave downward on the interval $\left(-\infty, \frac{1}{12}\right)$ and concave upward on the interval $\left(\frac{1}{12}, \infty\right)$. The inflection point of the graph is $\left(\frac{1}{12}, f\left(\frac{1}{12}\right)\right) = \left(\frac{1}{12}, \frac{359}{216}\right)$. The point $\left(\frac{2}{3}, f\left(\frac{2}{3}\right)\right) = \left(\frac{2}{3}, \frac{2}{27}\right)$ is a relative minimum and the point $\left(-\frac{1}{2}, f\left(-\frac{1}{2}\right)\right) = \left(-\frac{1}{2}, 3\frac{1}{4}\right)$ is a relative maximum.

115. D: The velocity v of the ball at any time t is the slope of the line tangent to the graph of h at time t. The slope of a line tangent to the curve $h = -16t^2 + 50t + 3$ is the same as h'.

$$h' = v = -32t + 50$$

When $t = 2$, the velocity of the ball is $-32(2) + 50 = -14$. The velocity is negative because the slope of the tangent line at $t = 2$ is negative; velocity has both magnitude and direction, so a velocity of –14 means that the velocity is 14 ft/s downward.

116. B: The manufacturer wishes to minimize the surface area A of the can while keeping its volume V fixed at $0.5\text{ L} = 500\text{ mL} = 500\text{ cm}^3$. The formula for the surface area of a cylinder is $A = 2\pi rh + 2\pi r^2$, and the formula for volume is $V = \pi r^2 h$. To combine the two formulas into one, solve the volume formula for r or h and substitute the resulting expression into the surface area formula for r or h. The volume of the cylinder is 500 cm^3, so $500 = \pi r^2 h \to h = \frac{500}{\pi r^2}$. Therefore, $A = 2\pi rh + 2\pi r^2 \to 2\pi r\left(\frac{500}{\pi r^2}\right) + 2\pi r^2 = \frac{1000}{r} + 2\pi r^2$. Find the critical point(s) by setting the first derivative equal to zero and solving for r. Note that r represents the radius of the can and must therefore be a positive number.

145

$$A = 1000r^{-1} + 2\pi r^2$$
$$A' = -1000r^{-2} + 4\pi r$$
$$0 = -\frac{1000}{r^2} + 4\pi r$$
$$\frac{1000}{r^2} = 4\pi r$$
$$1000 = 4\pi r^3$$
$$\sqrt[3]{\frac{1000}{4\pi}} = r \approx 4.3 \text{ cm}$$

So, when $r \approx 4.3$ cm, the minimum surface area is obtained. When the radius of the can is 4.30 cm, its height is $h \approx \frac{500}{\pi(4.30)^2} \approx 8.6$ cm, and surface area is approximately $\frac{1000}{4.3} + 2\pi(4.3)^2 \approx 348.73$ cm^2. Confirm that the surface area is greater when the radius is slightly smaller or larger than 4.3 cm. For instance, when $r = 4$ cm, the surface area is approximately 350.5 cm^2, and when $r = 4.5$ cm, the surface area is approximately 349.5 cm^2.

117. B: The area under curve $f(x)$ is $\int_1^2 \frac{1}{x} dx = [\ln x + C]_1^2 = [\ln(2) + C] - [\ln(1) + C] \approx 0.69$.

118. C: Partitioned into rectangles with length of 1, the left and right Riemann sums will establish upper and lower bounds for the true area.

The left Riemann sum: $20 + 25 + 28 + 30 + 29 + 26 + 22 + 16 + 12 + 10 + 10 + 13 = 241$

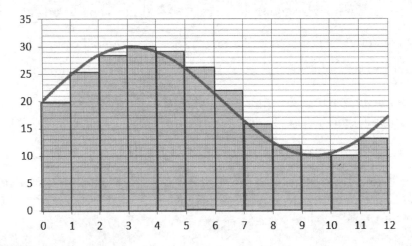

The right Riemann sum: $25 + 28 + 30 + 29 + 26 + 22 + 16 + 12 + 10 + 10 + 13 + 17 = 238$

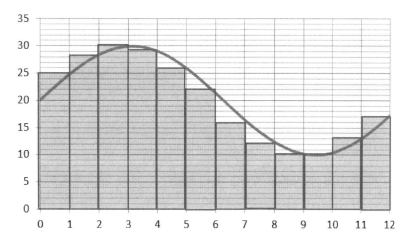

Thus, the bounds on A are: $238 < A < 241$.

119. A: $\int 3x^2 + 2x - 1 \, dx = \frac{3}{2+1}x^{(2+1)} + \frac{2}{1+1}x^{(1+1)} - x + C = x^3 + x^2 - x + C$

120. B: To find the integral, use substitution:

$$\int 3x^2 e^{x^3} \, dx \qquad \text{Let } u = x^3; \, du = 3x^2 dx$$

$$\int e^u \, du = e^u + C$$

$$= e^{x^3} + C$$

121. B: Find the points of intersection of the two graphs:

$$x^2 - 4 = -x + 2$$
$$x^2 + x - 6 = 0$$
$$(x + 3)(x - 2) = 0$$
$$x = -3, x = 2$$

So, the area is between the graphs on $[-3,2]$. To determine which of the graphs is the upper or lower bound, pick a test point in the interval. Using $x = 0$ as the test point:

$$y = 0^2 - 4 \qquad y = -0 + 2$$
$$y = -4 \qquad\quad y = 2$$

147

The finite region is bound at the top by the line $y = -x + 2$ and at the bottom by $y = x^2 - 4$, and the height of the region at point x is defined by $[(-x + 2) - (x^2 - 4)]$, so the area of the region is:

$$
\begin{aligned}
A &= \int_{-3}^{2} [(-x + 2) - (x^2 - 4)]dx \\
&= \int_{-3}^{2} (-x^2 - x + 6) \, dx \\
&= \left[-\frac{1}{3}x^3 - \frac{1}{2}x^2 + 6x + C \right]_{-3}^{2} \\
&= \left[-\frac{1}{3}(2)^3 - \frac{1}{2}(2)^2 + 6(2) + C \right] - \left[-\frac{1}{3}(-3)^3 - \frac{1}{2}(-3)^2 + 6(-3) + C \right] \\
&= \left[-\frac{8}{3} - 2 + 12 \right] - \left[9 - \frac{9}{2} - 18 \right] \\
&= \frac{22}{3} - \left(-\frac{27}{2} \right) \\
&= \frac{125}{6}
\end{aligned}
$$

122. C: The acceleration a of an object at time t is the derivative of the velocity v of the object with respect to time t, which is the derivative of the position x of the object with respect to time t. So, given the velocity of an object at time t, $x(t)$ can be found by taking the integral of the $v(t)$, and $a(t)$ can be found by taking the derivative of $v(t)$.

$$
\begin{aligned}
x(t) &= \int v(t)dt \\
&= \int (12t - t^2)dt \\
&= 6t^2 - \frac{1}{3}t^3 + c
\end{aligned}
$$

Since the position of the car at time 0 is 0:

$$
\begin{aligned}
0 &= x(0) \\
0 &= 6(0)^2 - \frac{1}{3}(0)^3 + c \\
0 &= 0 - 0 + c \\
0 &= c
\end{aligned}
$$

Therefore, $x(t) = 6t^2 - \frac{1}{3}t^3$.

The acceleration at time t is: $a(t) = v'(t) = 12 - 2t$.

Find the time at which the acceleration is equal to 0: $0 = 12 - 2t \rightarrow t = 6$. Then, find $x(6)$ to find the position of the car when the velocity is 0: $6(6)^2 - \frac{1}{3}(6)^3 = 216 - 72 = 144$.

123. D: To draw a box-and-whisker plot from the data, find the median, quartiles, and upper and lower limits.

```
3 | 6 7 9 9
4 | 2 3 8 8 9          Key
5 | 0 1 1 1 5 7      3 | 6 = 36
6 | 0 0 1 2 3
```

The median is $\frac{50+51}{2} = 50.5$, the lower quartile is $\frac{22+23}{2} = 22.5$, and the upper quartile is $\frac{57+60}{2} =$ 58.5. The box of the box-and-whisker plot goes through the quartiles, and a line through the box represents the median of the data. The whiskers extend from the box to the lower and upper limits, unless there are any outliers in the set. In this case, there are no outliers, so the box-and-whisker plot in choice A correctly represents the data set.

To draw a pie chart, find the percentage of data contained in each of the ranges shown. There are four out of twenty numbers between 30 and 39, inclusive, so the percentage shown in the pie chart for that range of data is $\frac{4}{20} \times 100\% = 20\%$; there are five values between 40 to 49, inclusive, so the percentage of data for that sector is $\frac{5}{20} \times 100\% = 25\%$; $\frac{6}{20} \times 100\% = 30\%$ of the data is within the range of 50-59, and $\frac{5}{20} \times 100\% = 25\%$ is within the range of 60-69. The pie chart shows the correct percentage of data in each category.

To draw a cumulative frequency histogram, find the cumulative frequency of the data.

Range	Frequency	Cumulative frequency
30-39	4	4
40-49	5	9
50-59	6	15
60-69	5	20

The histogram shows the correct cumulative frequencies.

Therefore, all of the graphs represent the data set.

124. B: A line graph is often used to show change over time. A Venn diagram shows the relationships among sets. A box-and-whisker plot displays how numeric data are distributed throughout the range. A pie chart shows the relationship of parts to a whole.

125. B: In choice A, the teacher surveys all the members of the population in which he is interested. However, since the response is voluntary, the survey is biased: the participants are self-selected rather than randomly selected. It may be that students who have a strong opinion are more likely to respond than those who are more neutral, and this would give the teacher a skewed perspective of student opinions. In choice B, students are randomly selected, so the sampling technique is not biased. In choice C, the student uses convenience sampling, which is a biased technique. For example, perhaps the student is in an honors class; his sampling method would not be representative of the entire class of eleventh graders, which includes both students who take and who do not take honors classes. Choice D also represents convenience sampling; only the opinions of parents in the PTA are examined, and these parents' opinions may not reflect the opinions of all parents of students at the school.

126. A: Nominal data are data that are collected which have no intrinsic quantity or order. For instance, a survey might ask the respondent to identify his or her gender. While it is possible to compare the relative frequency of each response (for example, "most of the respondents are women"), it is not possible to calculate the mean, which requires data to be numeric, or median, which requires data to be ordered. Interval data are both numeric and ordered, so mean and median can be determined, as can the mode, the interval within which there are the most data. Ordinal data has an inherent order, but there is not a set interval between two points. For example, a survey might ask the respondents whether they were very dissatisfied, dissatisfied, neutral, satisfied, or very satisfied with the customer service received. Since the data are not numeric, the mean cannot be calculated, but since ordering the data is possible, the median has context.

127. A: The average number of male students in the 11th and 12th grades is 125 (calculated as $\frac{131 + 119}{2}$). The number of Hispanic students at the school is 10% of 1219, which is 122 students (rounded up from 121.9). The difference in the number of male and female students at the school is $630 - 589 = 41$, and the difference in the number of 9th and 12th grade students at the school is $354 - 255 = 99$.

128. C: 52% of the student population is white. There are 630 female students at the school out of 1219 students, so the percentage of female students is $\frac{630}{1219} \times 100\% \approx 52\%$. The percentages rounded to the nearest whole number are the same.

129. D: 131 of 283 eleventh graders are male. Given that an 11th grader is chosen to attend the conference, the probability that a male is chosen is $\frac{\text{number of males}}{\text{number of 11th graders}} = \frac{131}{283} \approx 0.46$. Note that this is **NOT** the same question as one which asks for the probability of selecting at random from the school a male student who is in eleventh grade, which has a probability of $\frac{131}{1219} \approx 0.11$.

130. A: The range is the spread of the data. It can be calculated for each class by subtracting the lowest test score from the highest, or it can be determined visually from the graph. The difference between the highest and lowest test scores in class 1 is $98 - 23 = 75$ points. The range for each of the other classes is much smaller.

131. D: 75% of the data in a set is above the first quartile. Since the first quartile for this set is 73, there is a 75% chance that a student chosen at random from Class 2 scored above a 73.

132. C: The line through the center of the box represents the median. The median test score for classes 1 and 2 is 82.

Note that for class 1, the median is a better representation of the data than the mean. There are two outliers (points which lie outside of two standard deviations from the mean) which bring down the average test score. In cases such as this, the mean is not the best measure of central tendency.

133. D: Since there are 100 homes' market times represented in each set, the median time a home spends on the market is between the 50th and 51st data point in each set. The 50th and 51st data points for Zip Code 1 are six months and seven months, respectively, so the median time a house in Zip Code 1 spends on the market is between six and seven months (6.5 months), which by the realtor's definition of market time is a seven-month market time. The 50th and 51st data points for Zip Code 2 are both thirteen months, so the median time a house in Zip Code 2 spends on the market is thirteen months.

To find the mean market time for 100 houses, find the sum of the market times and divide by 100. If the frequency of a one-month market time is 9, the number 1 is added nine times (1×9), if frequency of a two-month market time is 10, the number 2 is added ten times (2×10), and so on. So, to find the average market time, divide by 100 the sum of the products of each market time and its corresponding frequency. For Zip Code 1, the mean market time is 7.38 months, which by the realtor's definition of market time is an eight-month market time. For Zip Code 2, the mean market time is 12.74, which by the realtor's definition of market time is a thirteen-month market time.

The mode market time is the market time for which the frequency is the highest. For Zip Code 1, the mode market time is three months, and for Zip Code 2, the mode market time is eleven months. Therefore, the median time a house spends on the market in Zip Code 1 is less than the mean time a house spends on the market in Zip Code 1.

134. C: The probability of an event is the number of possible occurrences of that event divided by the number of all possible outcomes. A camper who is at least eight years old can be eight, nine, or ten years old, so the probability of randomly selecting a camper at least eight years old is:

$$\frac{\text{number of eight-, nine-, and ten-year old campers}}{\text{total number of campers}} = \frac{14 + 12 + 10}{12 + 15 + 14 + 12 + 10} = \frac{36}{63} = \frac{4}{7}$$

135. B:

	Department 1	Department 2	Department 3	Total
Women	12	28	16	56
Men	18	14	15	47
Total	30	42	31	103

There are three ways in which two women from the same department can be selected: two women can be selected from the first department, or two women can be selected from the second department, or two women can be selected from the third department. The probability that two women are selected from Department 1 is $\frac{12}{103} \times \frac{11}{102} = \frac{132}{10,506}$, the probability that two women are selected from Department 2 is $\frac{28}{103} \times \frac{27}{102} = \frac{756}{10,506}$, and the probability that two women are selected from Department 3 is $\frac{16}{103} \times \frac{15}{102} = \frac{240}{10,506}$. Since any of these is a discrete possible outcome, the probability that two women will be selected from the same department is the sum of these outcomes: $\frac{132}{10,506} + \frac{756}{10,506} + \frac{240}{10,506} \approx 0.107$, or 10.7%.

136. B: Determine the probability of each option (if b = likes broccoli, c = likes carrots, and f = likes cauliflower).

For choice A, this is the total number of students in the broccoli circle of the Venn diagram divided by the total number of students surveyed:

$$P(b) = \frac{10 + 4 + 3 + 15}{90} = \frac{32}{90} \approx 35.6\%$$

For choice B, this is the total number of students in the carrots circle and also in at least one other circle divided by the total number in the carrots circle:

$$P(b \cup f|c) = \frac{15 + 3 + 6}{15 + 3 + 6 + 27} = \frac{24}{51} \approx 47.1\%$$

For choice C, this is the number of students in the intersection of all three circles divided by the total number in the overlap of the broccoli and cauliflower circles:

$$P(c|b \cap f) = \frac{3}{3 + 4} = \frac{3}{7} \approx 42.9\%$$

For choice D, this is the number of students outside of all the circles divided by the total number of students surveyed:

$$P([c \cup b \cup f]') = \frac{23}{90} \approx 25.6\%$$

137. C: Since each coin toss is an independent event, the probability of the compound event of flipping the coin three times is equal to the product of the probabilities of the individual events. For example, $P(HHH) = P(H) \times P(H) \times P(H)$, $P(HHT) = P(H) \times P(H) \times P(T)$, etc. When a coin is flipped three times, all of the possible outcomes are HHH, HHT, HTH, HTT, THH, THT, TTH, and TTT. Using the data from the all heads and all tails results, calculate an experimental probability $P(H)$:

$$P(\text{three heads}) = P(HHH) \qquad\qquad P(\text{no heads}) = P(TTT)$$
$$= P(H)P(H)P(H) \qquad\qquad\qquad = P(T)P(T)P(T)$$
$$= [P(H)]^3 \qquad\qquad\qquad\qquad = [P(T)]^3$$
$$[P(H)]^3 = \frac{30}{100} \qquad\qquad\qquad\qquad [P(T)]^3 = \frac{4}{100}$$
$$[P(H)] = \sqrt[3]{0.3} \approx 0.67 \qquad\qquad [P(T)] = \sqrt[3]{0.04} \approx 0.34$$
$$\qquad\qquad\qquad\qquad\qquad\qquad P(H) = 1 - P(T) \approx 0.66$$

Notice that these calculated values of $P(H)$ are approximately the same. Since 100 is a fairly large sample size for this kind of experiment, the approximation for $P(H)$ ought to be consistent for the compiled data set. Rather than calculating $P(H)$ using the data for one head and two heads, use the average calculated probability to confirm that the number of expected outcomes of one head and two head matches the number of actual outcomes.

$$P(\text{one head}) = P(HTT) + P(THT) + P(TTH) \qquad P(\text{two heads}) = P(HHT) + P(HTH) + P(THH)$$
$$= 3P(H)P(T)P(T) \qquad\qquad\qquad\qquad = 3P(H)P(H)P(T)$$
$$= 3P(H)[P(T)]^2 \qquad\qquad\qquad\qquad = 3[P(H)]^2 P(T)$$

The number of expected outcomes of getting one head in three coin flips out of 100 trials $100\{3(0.665)[(1 - 0.665)^2]\} \approx 22$, and the expected outcome getting of two heads in three coin flips out of 100 trials three flips is $100\{3(0.665)^2(1 - 0.665)\} \approx 44$. Since 22 and 44 are, in fact, the data obtained, 0.665 is indeed a good approximation for $P(H)$ when the coin used in this experiment is tossed.

138. D: A fair coin has a symmetrical binomial distribution which peaks in its center. Since choice B shows a skewed distribution for the fair coin, it cannot be the correct answer. From the frequency

152

histogram given for the misshapen coin, it is evident that the misshapen coin is more likely to land on heads. Therefore, it is more likely that ten coin flips would result in fewer tails than ten coin flips of a fair coin; consequently, the probability distribution for the misshapen coin would be higher than the fair coin's distribution toward the smaller number of tails. Choice A shows a probability distribution which peaks at a value of 5 and which is symmetrical with respect to the peak, which verifies that it cannot be correct. (Furthermore, in choice A, the sum of the probabilities shown for each number of tails for the misshapen coin is not equal to 1.) The distribution for the misshapen coin in choice C is skewed in the wrong direction, favoring tails instead of heads, and must therefore also be incorrect. Choice D shows the correct binomial distribution for the fair coin and the appropriate shift for the misshapen coin.

Another way to approach this question is to use the answer from the previous problem to determine the probability of obtaining particular events, such as no tails and no heads, and then compare those probabilities to the graphs. For example, for the misshapen coin:

$$P(0 \text{ tails}) = P(10 \text{ heads}) \approx (0.665)^{10} \approx 0.017$$
$$P(10 \text{ tails}) \approx (0.335)^{10} \approx 0.000018$$

For a fair coin:

$$P(0 \text{ tails}) = P(10 \text{ heads}) = P(10 \text{ tails}) = P(0 \text{ heads})$$
$$= (0.5)^{10} \approx 0.001$$

To find values other than these, it is helpful to use the binomial distribution formula $(_nC_r)p^r q^{n-r}$, where n is the number of trials, r is the number of successes, p is the probability of success, and q is the probability of failure. For this problem, obtaining tails is a success, and the probability of obtaining tails is $p = 0.33$ for the misshapen coin and $p = 0.5$ for the fair coin; so, $q = 0.67$ for the misshapen coin and $q = 0.5$ for the fair coin. To find the probability of, say, getting three tails for ten flips of the misshapen coin, find:

$$(_nC_r)p^r q^{n-r} = (_{10}C_3)(0.335)^3(0.665)^7 = \frac{10!}{3!\,7!}(0.335)^3(0.665)^7 \approx 0.259$$

The calculated probabilities match those shown in choice D.

139. C: When rolling two dice, there is only one way to roll a sum of two (rolling a 1 on each die) and twelve (rolling 6 on each die). In contrast, there are two ways to obtain a sum of three (rolling a 2 and 1 or a 1 and 2) and eleven (rolling a 5 and 6 or a 6 and 5), three ways to obtain a sum of four (1 and 3; 2 and 2; 3 and 1) or ten (4 and 6; 5 and 5; 6 and 4), and so on. Since the probability of obtaining each sum is inconsistent, choice C is not an appropriate simulation. Choice A is acceptable since the probability of picking A, 1, 2, 3, 4, 5, 6, 7, 8, 9, or J from the modified deck cards of cards is equally likely, each with a probability of $\frac{4}{52-8} = \frac{4}{44} = \frac{1}{11}$. Choice B is also acceptable since the computer randomly generates one number from eleven possible numbers, so the probability of generating any of the numbers is $\frac{1}{11}$.

140. C: There are 6 occurrences of aa, so the experimental probability of getting genotype aa is $\frac{6}{500} = 0.012$. There are 21 occurrences of bb, so the experimental probability of getting genotype bb is $\frac{21}{500} = 0.042$. The experimental probability of either getting genotype aa or bb is $0.012 + 0.042 = 0.054$. Multiply this experimental probability by 100,000 to find the number of individuals expected to be homozygous for either allele in a population of 100,000: $0.054 \times 100,000 = 5,400$.

141. D: A score of 85 is one standard deviation below the mean. Since approximately 68% of the data is within one standard deviation of the mean, about 32% (100%-68%) of the data is outside of one standard deviation within the mean. Normally distributed data is symmetric about the mean, which means that about 16% of the data lies below one standard deviation below the mean and about 16% of data lies above one standard deviation above the mean. Therefore, approximately 16% of individuals have IQs less than 85, while approximately 84% of the population has an IQ of at least 85. Since 84% of 300 is 252, about 252 people from the selected group have IQs of at least 85.

142. C: There are nine ways to assign the first digit since it can be any of the numbers 1-9. There are nine ways to assign the second digit since it can be any digit 0-9 EXCEPT for the digit assigned in place 1. There are eight ways to assign the third number since there are ten digits, two of which have already been assigned. There are seven ways to assign the fourth number, six ways to assign the fifth, five ways to assign the sixth, and four ways to assign the seventh. So, the number of combinations is $9 \times 9 \times 8 \times 7 \times 6 \times 5 \times 4 = 544,320$.

Another way to approach the problem is to notice that the arrangement of nine digits in the last six places is a sequence without repetition, or a permutation. (Note: this may be called a partial permutation since all of the elements of the set need not be used.) The number of possible sequences of a fixed length r of elements taken from a given set of size n is permutation $_nP_r = \frac{n!}{(n-r)!}$. So, the number of ways to arrange the last six digits is $_9P_6 = \frac{9!}{(9-6)!} = \frac{9!}{3!} = 60,480$. Multiply this number by nine since there are nine possibilities for the first digit of the phone number. $_9P_6 \times 9 = 544,320$.

143. B: If each of the four groups in the class of twenty will contain three boys and two girls, there must be twelve boys and eight girls in the class. The number of ways the teacher can select three boys from a group of twelve boys is:

$$_{12}C_3 = \frac{12!}{3!\,(12-3)!} = \frac{12!}{3!\,9!} = \frac{12 \times 11 \times 10 \times 9!}{3!\,9!} = \frac{12 \times 11 \times 10}{3 \times 2 \times 1} = 220$$

The number of ways she can select two girls from a group of eight girls is:

$$_8C_2 = \frac{8!}{2!\,(8-2)!} = \frac{8!}{2!\,6!} = \frac{8 \times 7 \times 6!}{2!\,6!} = \frac{8 \times 7}{2 \times 1} = 28$$

Since each combination of boys can be paired with each combination of girls, the number of group combinations is $220 \times 28 = 6,160$.

144. B: One way to approach this problem is to first consider the number of arrangements of the five members of the family if Tasha (T) and Mac (M) must sit together. Treat them as a unit seated in a fixed location at the table; then arrange the other three family members (A, B, and C):

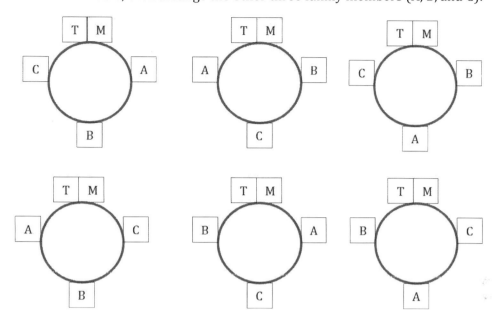

There are six ways to arrange four units around a circle as shown. (Any other arrangement would be a rotation in which the elements in the same order and would therefore not be a unique arrangement.) Note that there are $(n-1)!$ ways to arrange n units around a circle for $n > 1$.

Of course, Mac and Tasha are not actually a single unit. They would still be sitting beside each other if they were to trade seats, so there are twelve arrangements in which the two are seated next to one another. In all other arrangements of the five family members, they are separated. Therefore, to find the number of arrangements in which Tasha and Mac are not sitting together, subtract twelve from the possible arrangement of five units around a circle: $(5-1)! - 12 = 24 - 12 = 12$.

145. A: The recursive definition of the sequence gives the first term of the series, $a_1 = -1$. The definition also defines each term in the series as the sum of the previous term and 2. Therefore, the second term in the series is $-1 + 2 = 1$, the third term in the series is $1 + 2 = 3$, and so on.

n	a_n
1	-1
2	1
3	3

The relationship between n and a_n is linear, so the equation of the sequence can be found in the same way as the equation of a line. The value of a_n increases by two each time the value of n increases by 1.

n	$2n$	a_n
1	2	-1
2	4	1
3	6	3

155

Since the difference in $2n$ and a_n is 3, $a_n = 2n - 3$.

n	$2n - 3$	a_n
1	$2 - 3$	-1
2	$4 - 3$	1
3	$6 - 3$	3

146. B: The series is an infinite geometric series, the sum of which can be found by using the formula $\sum_{n=0}^{\infty} ar^n = \frac{a}{1-r}$, $|r| < 1$ where a is the first term in the series and r is the ratio between successive terms. In the series $200 + 100 + 50 + 25 + \cdots$, $a = 200$ and $r = \frac{1}{2}$. So, the sum of the series is:

$$\frac{200}{1 - \frac{1}{2}} = \frac{200}{\frac{1}{2}} = 400$$

147. A: The sum of two vectors is equal to the sum of their components. Using component-wise addition,

$$v + w = \big((4 - 3), (3 + 4)\big) = (1, 7)$$

To multiply a vector by a scalar, multiply each component by that scalar. Using component-wise scalar multiplication,

$$2(1, 7) = (2 \times 1, 2 \times 7) = (2, 14)$$

148. A: First, subtract the matrices in parentheses, then multiply the resulting matrices together:

$$[2 \quad 0 \quad -5]\begin{bmatrix} (4 - 3) \\ (2 - 5) \\ (-1 - (-5)) \end{bmatrix} = [2 \quad 0 \quad -5]\begin{bmatrix} 1 \\ -3 \\ 4 \end{bmatrix}$$
$$= [(2)(1) + (0)(-3) + (-5)(4)]$$
$$= [-18]$$

(Note that the product of a 1×3 matrix and a 3×1 matrix, in that order, is a 1×1 matrix. If the order was reversed, the product would be a 3×3 matrix)

149. B: The table below shows the intersections of each set with each of the other sets.

Set	{2,4,6,8,10,12, ...}	{1,2,3,4,6,12}	{1,2,4,9}
{2,4,6,8,10,12, ... }	{2,4,6,8,10,12, ...}	{2,4,6,12}	{2,4}
{1,2,3,4,6,12}	{2,4,6,12}	{1,2,3,4,6,12}	{1,2,4}
{1,2,4,9}	{2,4}	{1,2,4}	{1,2,4,9}

Notice that {2,4} is a subset of {2,4,6,12} and {1,2,4}. So, the intersection of {1,2,4,9} and the even integers is a subset of the intersection of the even integers and the factors of twelve, and the intersection of the set of even integers and {1,2,4,9} is a subset of the intersection of {1,2,4,9} and the factors of twelve. So, while it is not possible to determine which set is A and which is B, set C must be the set of factors of twelve: {1,2,3,4,6,12}.

150. D: Use a Venn diagram to help organize the given information. Start by filling in the space where the three circles intersect: Jenny tutored three students in all three areas. Use that information to fill in the spaces where two circles intersect: for example, she tutored four students in chemistry and for the ACT, and three of those were students she tutored in all three areas, so one student was tutored in chemistry and for the ACT but not for math. Once the diagram is completed, add the number of students who were tutored in all areas to the number of students tutored in only two of the three areas to the number of students tutored in only one area. The total number of students tutored was $3 + 2 + 2 + 1 + 3 + 2 + 1 = 14$.

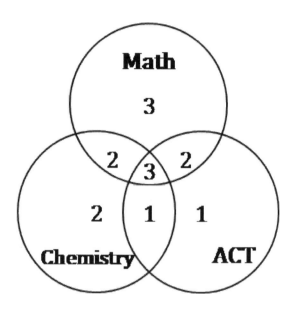

How to Overcome Test Anxiety

Just the thought of taking a test is enough to make most people a little nervous. A test is an important event that can have a long-term impact on your future, so it's important to take it seriously and it's natural to feel anxious about performing well. But just because anxiety is normal, that doesn't mean that it's helpful in test taking, or that you should simply accept it as part of your life. Anxiety can have a variety of effects. These effects can be mild, like making you feel slightly nervous, or severe, like blocking your ability to focus or remember even a simple detail.

If you experience test anxiety—whether severe or mild—it's important to know how to beat it. To discover this, first you need to understand what causes test anxiety.

Causes of Test Anxiety

While we often think of anxiety as an uncontrollable emotional state, it can actually be caused by simple, practical things. One of the most common causes of test anxiety is that a person does not feel adequately prepared for their test. This feeling can be the result of many different issues such as poor study habits or lack of organization, but the most common culprit is time management. Starting to study too late, failing to organize your study time to cover all of the material, or being distracted while you study will mean that you're not well prepared for the test. This may lead to cramming the night before, which will cause you to be physically and mentally exhausted for the test. Poor time management also contributes to feelings of stress, fear, and hopelessness as you realize you are not well prepared but don't know what to do about it.

Other times, test anxiety is not related to your preparation for the test but comes from unresolved fear. This may be a past failure on a test, or poor performance on tests in general. It may come from comparing yourself to others who seem to be performing better or from the stress of living up to expectations. Anxiety may be driven by fears of the future—how failure on this test would affect your educational and career goals. These fears are often completely irrational, but they can still negatively impact your test performance.

> **Review Video: <u>3 Reasons You Have Test Anxiety</u>**
> Visit mometrix.com/academy and enter code: 428468

Elements of Test Anxiety

As mentioned earlier, test anxiety is considered to be an emotional state, but it has physical and mental components as well. Sometimes you may not even realize that you are suffering from test anxiety until you notice the physical symptoms. These can include trembling hands, rapid heartbeat, sweating, nausea, and tense muscles. Extreme anxiety may lead to fainting or vomiting. Obviously, any of these symptoms can have a negative impact on testing. It is important to recognize them as soon as they begin to occur so that you can address the problem before it damages your performance.

> **Review Video: 3 Ways to Tell You Have Test Anxiety**
> Visit mometrix.com/academy and enter code: 927847

The mental components of test anxiety include trouble focusing and inability to remember learned information. During a test, your mind is on high alert, which can help you recall information and stay focused for an extended period of time. However, anxiety interferes with your mind's natural processes, causing you to blank out, even on the questions you know well. The strain of testing during anxiety makes it difficult to stay focused, especially on a test that may take several hours. Extreme anxiety can take a huge mental toll, making it difficult not only to recall test information but even to understand the test questions or pull your thoughts together.

> **Review Video: How Test Anxiety Affects Memory**
> Visit mometrix.com/academy and enter code: 609003

Effects of Test Anxiety

Test anxiety is like a disease—if left untreated, it will get progressively worse. Anxiety leads to poor performance, and this reinforces the feelings of fear and failure, which in turn lead to poor performances on subsequent tests. It can grow from a mild nervousness to a crippling condition. If allowed to progress, test anxiety can have a big impact on your schooling, and consequently on your future.

Test anxiety can spread to other parts of your life. Anxiety on tests can become anxiety in any stressful situation, and blanking on a test can turn into panicking in a job situation. But fortunately, you don't have to let anxiety rule your testing and determine your grades. There are a number of relatively simple steps you can take to move past anxiety and function normally on a test and in the rest of life.

> **Review Video: How Test Anxiety Impacts Your Grades**
> Visit mometrix.com/academy and enter code: 939819

Physical Steps for Beating Test Anxiety

While test anxiety is a serious problem, the good news is that it can be overcome. It doesn't have to control your ability to think and remember information. While it may take time, you can begin taking steps today to beat anxiety.

Just as your first hint that you may be struggling with anxiety comes from the physical symptoms, the first step to treating it is also physical. Rest is crucial for having a clear, strong mind. If you are tired, it is much easier to give in to anxiety. But if you establish good sleep habits, your body and mind will be ready to perform optimally, without the strain of exhaustion. Additionally, sleeping well helps you to retain information better, so you're more likely to recall the answers when you see the test questions.

Getting good sleep means more than going to bed on time. It's important to allow your brain time to relax. Take study breaks from time to time so it doesn't get overworked, and don't study right before bed. Take time to rest your mind before trying to rest your body, or you may find it difficult to fall asleep.

> **Review Video: The Importance of Sleep for Your Brain**
> Visit mometrix.com/academy and enter code: 319338

Along with sleep, other aspects of physical health are important in preparing for a test. Good nutrition is vital for good brain function. Sugary foods and drinks may give a burst of energy but this burst is followed by a crash, both physically and emotionally. Instead, fuel your body with protein and vitamin-rich foods.

Also, drink plenty of water. Dehydration can lead to headaches and exhaustion, especially if your brain is already under stress from the rigors of the test. Particularly if your test is a long one, drink water during the breaks. And if possible, take an energy-boosting snack to eat between sections.

> **Review Video: How Diet Can Affect your Mood**
> Visit mometrix.com/academy and enter code: 624317

Along with sleep and diet, a third important part of physical health is exercise. Maintaining a steady workout schedule is helpful, but even taking 5-minute study breaks to walk can help get your blood pumping faster and clear your head. Exercise also releases endorphins, which contribute to a positive feeling and can help combat test anxiety.

When you nurture your physical health, you are also contributing to your mental health. If your body is healthy, your mind is much more likely to be healthy as well. So take time to rest, nourish your body with healthy food and water, and get moving as much as possible. Taking these physical steps will make you stronger and more able to take the mental steps necessary to overcome test anxiety.

Mometrix

Mental Steps for Beating Test Anxiety

Working on the mental side of test anxiety can be more challenging, but as with the physical side, there are clear steps you can take to overcome it. As mentioned earlier, test anxiety often stems from lack of preparation, so the obvious solution is to prepare for the test. Effective studying may be the most important weapon you have for beating test anxiety, but you can and should employ several other mental tools to combat fear.

First, boost your confidence by reminding yourself of past success—tests or projects that you aced. If you're putting as much effort into preparing for this test as you did for those, there's no reason you should expect to fail here. Work hard to prepare; then trust your preparation.

Second, surround yourself with encouraging people. It can be helpful to find a study group, but be sure that the people you're around will encourage a positive attitude. If you spend time with others who are anxious or cynical, this will only contribute to your own anxiety. Look for others who are motivated to study hard from a desire to succeed, not from a fear of failure.

Third, reward yourself. A test is physically and mentally tiring, even without anxiety, and it can be helpful to have something to look forward to. Plan an activity following the test, regardless of the outcome, such as going to a movie or getting ice cream.

When you are taking the test, if you find yourself beginning to feel anxious, remind yourself that you know the material. Visualize successfully completing the test. Then take a few deep, relaxing breaths and return to it. Work through the questions carefully but with confidence, knowing that you are capable of succeeding.

Developing a healthy mental approach to test taking will also aid in other areas of life. Test anxiety affects more than just the actual test—it can be damaging to your mental health and even contribute to depression. It's important to beat test anxiety before it becomes a problem for more than testing.

> **Review Video: Test Anxiety and Depression**
> Visit mometrix.com/academy and enter code: 904704

Study Strategy

Being prepared for the test is necessary to combat anxiety, but what does being prepared look like? You may study for hours on end and still not feel prepared. What you need is a strategy for test prep. The next few pages outline our recommended steps to help you plan out and conquer the challenge of preparation.

STEP 1: SCOPE OUT THE TEST

Learn everything you can about the format (multiple choice, essay, etc.) and what will be on the test. Gather any study materials, course outlines, or sample exams that may be available. Not only will this help you to prepare, but knowing what to expect can help to alleviate test anxiety.

STEP 2: MAP OUT THE MATERIAL

Look through the textbook or study guide and make note of how many chapters or sections it has. Then divide these over the time you have. For example, if a book has 15 chapters and you have five days to study, you need to cover three chapters each day. Even better, if you have the time, leave an extra day at the end for overall review after you have gone through the material in depth.

If time is limited, you may need to prioritize the material. Look through it and make note of which sections you think you already have a good grasp on, and which need review. While you are studying, skim quickly through the familiar sections and take more time on the challenging parts. Write out your plan so you don't get lost as you go. Having a written plan also helps you feel more in control of the study, so anxiety is less likely to arise from feeling overwhelmed at the amount to cover.

STEP 3: GATHER YOUR TOOLS

Decide what study method works best for you. Do you prefer to highlight in the book as you study and then go back over the highlighted portions? Or do you type out notes of the important information? Or is it helpful to make flashcards that you can carry with you? Assemble the pens, index cards, highlighters, post-it notes, and any other materials you may need so you won't be distracted by getting up to find things while you study.

If you're having a hard time retaining the information or organizing your notes, experiment with different methods. For example, try color-coding by subject with colored pens, highlighters, or post-it notes. If you learn better by hearing, try recording yourself reading your notes so you can listen while in the car, working out, or simply sitting at your desk. Ask a friend to quiz you from your flashcards, or try teaching someone the material to solidify it in your mind.

STEP 4: CREATE YOUR ENVIRONMENT

It's important to avoid distractions while you study. This includes both the obvious distractions like visitors and the subtle distractions like an uncomfortable chair (or a too-comfortable couch that makes you want to fall asleep). Set up the best study environment possible: good lighting and a comfortable work area. If background music helps you focus, you may want to turn it on, but otherwise keep the room quiet. If you are using a computer to take notes, be sure you don't have any other windows open, especially applications like social media, games, or anything else that could distract you. Silence your phone and turn off notifications. Be sure to keep water close by so you stay hydrated while you study (but avoid unhealthy drinks and snacks).

Also, take into account the best time of day to study. Are you freshest first thing in the morning? Try to set aside some time then to work through the material. Is your mind clearer in the afternoon or evening? Schedule your study session then. Another method is to study at the same time of day that you will take the test, so that your brain gets used to working on the material at that time and will be ready to focus at test time.

STEP 5: STUDY!

Once you have done all the study preparation, it's time to settle into the actual studying. Sit down, take a few moments to settle your mind so you can focus, and begin to follow your study plan. Don't give in to distractions or let yourself procrastinate. This is your time to prepare so you'll be ready to fearlessly approach the test. Make the most of the time and stay focused.

Of course, you don't want to burn out. If you study too long you may find that you're not retaining the information very well. Take regular study breaks. For example, taking five minutes out of every hour to walk briskly, breathing deeply and swinging your arms, can help your mind stay fresh.

As you get to the end of each chapter or section, it's a good idea to do a quick review. Remind yourself of what you learned and work on any difficult parts. When you feel that you've mastered the material, move on to the next part. At the end of your study session, briefly skim through your notes again.

But while review is helpful, cramming last minute is NOT. If at all possible, work ahead so that you won't need to fit all your study into the last day. Cramming overloads your brain with more information than it can process and retain, and your tired mind may struggle to recall even previously learned information when it is overwhelmed with last-minute study. Also, the urgent nature of cramming and the stress placed on your brain contribute to anxiety. You'll be more likely to go to the test feeling unprepared and having trouble thinking clearly.

So don't cram, and don't stay up late before the test, even just to review your notes at a leisurely pace. Your brain needs rest more than it needs to go over the information again. In fact, plan to finish your studies by noon or early afternoon the day before the test. Give your brain the rest of the day to relax or focus on other things, and get a good night's sleep. Then you will be fresh for the test and better able to recall what you've studied.

STEP 6: TAKE A PRACTICE TEST

Many courses offer sample tests, either online or in the study materials. This is an excellent resource to check whether you have mastered the material, as well as to prepare for the test format and environment.

Check the test format ahead of time: the number of questions, the type (multiple choice, free response, etc.), and the time limit. Then create a plan for working through them. For example, if you have 30 minutes to take a 60-question test, your limit is 30 seconds per question. Spend less time on the questions you know well so that you can take more time on the difficult ones.

If you have time to take several practice tests, take the first one open book, with no time limit. Work through the questions at your own pace and make sure you fully understand them. Gradually work up to taking a test under test conditions: sit at a desk with all study materials put away and set a timer. Pace yourself to make sure you finish the test with time to spare and go back to check your answers if you have time.

After each test, check your answers. On the questions you missed, be sure you understand why you missed them. Did you misread the question (tests can use tricky wording)? Did you forget the information? Or was it something you hadn't learned? Go back and study any shaky areas that the practice tests reveal.

Taking these tests not only helps with your grade, but also aids in combating test anxiety. If you're already used to the test conditions, you're less likely to worry about it, and working through tests until you're scoring well gives you a confidence boost. Go through the practice tests until you feel comfortable, and then you can go into the test knowing that you're ready for it.

Test Tips

On test day, you should be confident, knowing that you've prepared well and are ready to answer the questions. But aside from preparation, there are several test day strategies you can employ to maximize your performance.

First, as stated before, get a good night's sleep the night before the test (and for several nights before that, if possible). Go into the test with a fresh, alert mind rather than staying up late to study.

Try not to change too much about your normal routine on the day of the test. It's important to eat a nutritious breakfast, but if you normally don't eat breakfast at all, consider eating just a protein bar. If you're a coffee drinker, go ahead and have your normal coffee. Just make sure you time it so that the caffeine doesn't wear off right in the middle of your test. Avoid sugary beverages, and drink enough water to stay hydrated but not so much that you need a restroom break 10 minutes into the test. If your test isn't first thing in the morning, consider going for a walk or doing a light workout before the test to get your blood flowing.

Allow yourself enough time to get ready, and leave for the test with plenty of time to spare so you won't have the anxiety of scrambling to arrive in time. Another reason to be early is to select a good seat. It's helpful to sit away from doors and windows, which can be distracting. Find a good seat, get out your supplies, and settle your mind before the test begins.

When the test begins, start by going over the instructions carefully, even if you already know what to expect. Make sure you avoid any careless mistakes by following the directions.

Then begin working through the questions, pacing yourself as you've practiced. If you're not sure on an answer, don't spend too much time on it, and don't let it shake your confidence. Either skip it and come back later, or eliminate as many wrong answers as possible and guess among the remaining ones. Don't dwell on these questions as you continue—put them out of your mind and focus on what lies ahead.

Be sure to read all of the answer choices, even if you're sure the first one is the right answer. Sometimes you'll find a better one if you keep reading. But don't second-guess yourself if you do immediately know the answer. Your gut instinct is usually right. Don't let test anxiety rob you of the information you know.

If you have time at the end of the test (and if the test format allows), go back and review your answers. Be cautious about changing any, since your first instinct tends to be correct, but make sure you didn't misread any of the questions or accidentally mark the wrong answer choice. Look over any you skipped and make an educated guess.

At the end, leave the test feeling confident. You've done your best, so don't waste time worrying about your performance or wishing you could change anything. Instead, celebrate the successful completion of this test. And finally, use this test to learn how to deal with anxiety even better next time.

> **Review Video: 5 Tips to Beat Test Anxiety**
> Visit mometrix.com/academy and enter code: 570656

Important Qualification

Not all anxiety is created equal. If your test anxiety is causing major issues in your life beyond the classroom or testing center, or if you are experiencing troubling physical symptoms related to your anxiety, it may be a sign of a serious physiological or psychological condition. If this sounds like your situation, we strongly encourage you to seek professional help.

Thank You

We at Mometrix would like to extend our heartfelt thanks to you, our friend and patron, for allowing us to play a part in your journey. It is a privilege to serve people from all walks of life who are unified in their commitment to building the best future they can for themselves.

The preparation you devote to these important testing milestones may be the most valuable educational opportunity you have for making a real difference in your life. We encourage you to put your heart into it—that feeling of succeeding, overcoming, and yes, conquering will be well worth the hours you've invested.

We want to hear your story, your struggles and your successes, and if you see any opportunities for us to improve our materials so we can help others even more effectively in the future, please share that with us as well. **The team at Mometrix would be absolutely thrilled to hear from you!** So please, send us an email (support@mometrix.com) and let's stay in touch.

> **If you'd like some additional help, check out these other resources we offer for your exam:**
> **http://MometrixFlashcards.com/OAE**

Additional Bonus Material

Due to our efforts to try to keep this book to a manageable length, we've created a link that will give you access to all of your additional bonus material:

mometrix.com/bonus948/oaemath